Ancient Olympic Games

Ancient Olympic Games

Banned • Revived • Roaring

Agha Rizvi

GenNext Publication

First Published, 2017

Published by

GenNext Publication
5, Ansari Road
Daryaganj, New Delhi-110002
Phone: 9811692060
E-mail: gennextpublication@hotmail.com

Printed at: G. Print Process, Delhi.

Cataloging in Publication Data—DK
Courtesy: D.K. Agencies (P) Ltd. <docinfo@dkagencies.com>

Rizvi, Agha, author.
Ancient Olympic games : banned, revived, roaring / Agha Rizvi.
pages cm
Includes bibliographical references.
ISBN: 978-93-5324-114-8

1. Olympic games (Ancient) 2. Olympics—History. I. Title.

GV23.R59 2017 DDC 796.4809 23

Contents

Synopsis

This book portrays on a larger canvas the glories, trials and tribulations of the ancient Olympic Games. No other book has ever provided such a thorough documentation of that ancient heritage.

The book opens with the chapter 'The Legendary Origin of the Olympic Games', which reaches back to pre-historic times. The Olympic 'concept' has been exhaustively traced drawing heavily from the authoritative versions of the Greek myths and original sources such as Homer's 'Iliad' and 'Odyssey', historical writings of Herodatus and Hesiod, Pausania's travelogues, Pindar's Odes, to name but a few.

A separate chapter is devoted to Olympia, the site of the ancient Olympic Games, describing vividly the lay-out and the environs of the Altis, - the sacred precinct. The next chapter exclusively deals with the organisation, conduct and development of the Olympic Games in ancient times under the heading 'Olympic Regimen in Ancient Times'. Deeds and achievements of some of the outstanding performers, viz., Polydamas, Theogenes, Euthymus, Flaucus, Milo, Pisidores, have been recalled in detail in the chapter captioned 'Heroes of Ancient Olympics' which should make a very interesting reading.

When Greece came under the sway of the Romans, the Games, slowly, yet surely, lost the sanctity and reverence surrounding them and were ultimately banned by the Roman Emperor Theodosius I in 393 AD. The circumstances culminating into the suspension of the Games form the theme of the fifth chapter. Then follows the story of how the Games were revived in the Nineteenth Century by

Baron de Coubertine after several earlier attempts had ended in failure.

Even though the Games were revived in 1896, certain pulls and pressures coupled with indifferent handling of subsequent Olympics by the host countries, the future of the Olympic movement seemed to be far from secure. All such factors have been bunched under the caption: "The Teething Troubles".

Curiously enough, the marathon race, a glamour attraction and a prestigious event, played a significant role in laying a solid foundation for the Games. How this came to pass has been brought out in a separate chapter: "The Marathon Story".

Having surveyed the scenario thus far it was considered appropriate to devote an entire chapter to the fundamentals of the various track and field events and present some vital information about the Olympic set-up and organisation in the next two chapters.

Then begins the cavalcade of Olympic Games with a separate chapter earmarked for each Olympics of the modern era, from the first in Athens in 1896 to the eleventh in Berlin in 1936 where the organisation and conduct of the Games was perfected and thus securing the future of the Olympic Games. The chapters recount the highlights of each Games, touching on the historical background and the pomp and pageantry in which they were held. Performances of all the participating countries have been highlighted at appropriate places and in proper perspective.

Preface

Mere mention of the word 'Olympics' recalls to mind something great, grand and gorgeous; colossal and celestial at the same time. No wonder that from time immemorial, there has hardly ever been an event which could hold a candle to the Olympic Games in length of existence, force of impact and the enthusiastic interest it stirs up of the entire civilized world. Indeed, there is no sporting occasion quite like the Olympic Games. No other event can capture its international appeal and its intensity of competition in such a range of sports. No wonder, therefore, that the Olympic Games should hit the headlines almost daily during every Olympic year. There is, however, all too little literature particularly on that glorious heritage from ancient Greek civilization to which the world pays homage by organizing the modern Olympic Games.

In this back-drop it is an intriguing mystery why this fascinating subject of ancient Olympics has not fired the imagination of our potential sports scribes. Apart from stray pictorials, I have seen only one book by an Indian author, *Story of the Olympic Games* by Melville De Mello, published by National Book Trust way back in 1972. But that book describes only the modern Olympic games, i.e., from 1896 onwards and not the ancient Olympics which are summarily mentioned in not more than a couple of pages.

Our subject of study is the Ancient Olympic Games; when, where and how they were held; the respect and reverence they enjoyed and then after centuries of its continuous, glorious run the circumstances under which they were banned. And then again, after 1500 years, efforts to rejuvenate that ancient revered sporting institution fructified and in 1896 A.D. saw the re-emergence of the Ancient Olympic Games.

The re-emergence of the Ancient Olympic Games in the modern era was not an overnight affair. It took forty long years (1896 to 1936), sustaining the initial hiccups to find a firm foot- hold, promising a secure future for all times to come. It was at the Berlin Olympic Games in 1936 that perfection in the conduct and organization of Olympic Games was attained so that one can rejoice that the glorious heritage of modern Olympic Games has once again come alive.

To say that the relevant, authentic material on the Ancient Olympic Games from original sources is hard to get will be a truth, though not the whole of it and also not exactly either. The Greek historical writings that have come down to us are rich and imposing; it is another matter though that what we are looking for may be elusive.

Two great works, *'Works and Days'* and '*Theogony'* by the 8th Century B.C. Greek poet Hesiod are diverse in nature, the one dealing with agricultural seasons and the other concerning origin of the world and the genealogies of the gods, but both have references to the 'Games'. Another Greek historian, Herodotus called the Father of History (485– 425 B.C.) and famous for his work '*History*' has at several places referred to Olympia and 'The Games'. Then there was Pindar (518 – 438 B.C.) the great Greek lyric poet famous for his 'odes' and noted for his '*Epinikia*' containing odes commemorating victories in the Greek Games i.e., in addition to the Olympic Games, Pindar has repeatedly referred to the Pythian, the Nemian and the Isthemian Games as well which were regular features in ancient Greece.

Odyssey and Iliad, the two classic epics attributed to Homer, the one describing the ten-year homeward wanderings of Odysseus and the other describing the siege of Troy, both have references to the Olympic Games, scattered though.

Pausanias, in the 2nd century A.D. was a Greek historian as also a geographer. His *Description of Greece* gives a valuable account of the topography of ancient Greece. He was a prolific writer. His travelogues, translated into English by J.W. Frazer, run in six hefty volumes, and have some meaningful references to the Olympic Games. But it has to be kept in mind that Pausanias traveled Greece in

2nd Century A.D. when Greece was already under the dominance of Romans because of which the decadence in the Games had already crept in.

In all these and other Greek writings of yore, the references to the ancient Olympic Games are so far and wide that if you scan through 500 pages you will indeed be lucky, if in the bargain, you get a line or two relevant to your story.

The exercise of sifting the relevant material has been arduous, time consuming; interesting nevertheless. H.G. Wells, in his *Outline of History* aptly sums up : 'The history of Greece lacks the fixity of records'.

So now, on to the text of 'Ancient Olympic Games' Banned * Revived * Roaring'.

Author

1

The Legendary Origin

The history of the Olympic Games is replete with fascinating tales – tales unfolding splendour, spectacle, pageantry and the glory that is necessarily associated with sports. In this fast changing world, where divergent views and conflicting interests have been the order of the day, the cavalcade of Olympic Games has been unceasingly inspiring mankind and promoting goodwill and friendship among the peoples of the world through the ages.

Despite so many modern researches, the origin of the Olympic Games is still burried in obscurity. It is, however, universally acknowledged that the first Olympics was held in 776 BC although there are positive indications that athletic competitions were staged centuries earlier than the accepted date. The origin of Olympics, no doubt, dates back to pre-historic times, with the highly imaginative Greeks spinning and concocting many a fabulous tale to explain its origin.

A legend has it that Heracles (to wit, the Hercules whom we know better) was, as a penance to his misdeeds, entrusted with the almost impossible job of cleaning the stables of Augeas, son of Helius, who was the king of the Epeans in Elis. Augeas owned a huge herd which comprised 3,000 oxen, including 12 white bulls sacred to the sun. The whole lot was housed in a stable which had not been cleaned in 30 years. As one of his labours for Eurystheus, Heracles undertook to clean the stable in one day and Augeas, by way of a bet, agreed to pay him one-tenth of his herd as commission if Heracles could fulfil the task in the time stipulated. Phyleus, son of Augeas, was made to stand as a witness to the deal.

Heracles accomplished the task with consummate ease by changing the course of the river Alpheus to run through the stable. Having won, he demanded his share of the bet. Augeas, however, did not like Heracles' modus operandi and refused to honour his agreement on the ground that, in the first instance, Heracles had been commanded to carry out this task by Eurystheus and, furthermore, he had been substantially assisted by the river gods. When Phyleus ventured to intervene by reminding the obligations of the bet, Augeas flared up and banished him. This infuriated Heracles. He gathered a force and killed Augeas along with his other sons and made Phyleus ruler of the kingdom. In order to commemorate his feats and the acquisition of the empire, as also by way of penance, Heracles held the first ever Olympic Games in 1222 BC.

Another version, with a bit of historical basis to vouch for its authenticity, would like us to believe that Cleosthenes of Pisa and Lycurgus, the great Spartan formulator of law who commanded great respect because of his own exemplary conduct and background, shared with Iphitus, the King of Elis, the grave concern over wars between states which were slowly, yet surely, destroying the country's unity. Iphitus, to get rid of the crisis and the distress pervading his country, decided to consult the Oracle and was advised to revive the games at Olympia so that peace might dawn. His messenger to the Delphic Oracle returned with the command: "The Olympic festival should be restored; for its neglect had brought upon the Greeks the wrath of Jupiter, to whom it had been dedicated, and of Heracles, by whom it had been instituted, and that a cessation of arms must, therefore, be proclaimed for all cities desirous of partaking in it".

The King, accordingly restored the festival in 884 BC though the epoch of Olympiads took place 108 years afterwards, i.e., in 776 BC. The words 'revive' and 'restore' in this context, bear a special significance inasmuch as they are a pointer to the fact that the games had been held earlier also. The Greek states didn't, however, enjoy lasting peace, but during the games a truce was declared and all athletes were given safe conduct through enemy territory. From that day on, the Olympics have been a symbol of peace and international goodwill.

The Greek mythology unfolds another legend according to which Zeus and Kronos, the mightiest of the gods, wrestled for the possession of the earth on the high peaks above; the games and religious celebrations held later in the valley below were in commemoration of the victory of Zeus.

Yet another legend that of Pelops, with a bizarre touch, is full of romance and adventure. Once again the river Alpheus provides the background to the story – this time of a King of Elis, Oenomaus, with a beautiful daughter named Hippodemia. Either because of incestuous love for her or because an Oracle had foretold he would die at the hands of his son-in-law, Oenomaus just avoided giving Hippodemia in marriage. To hide his guilt, or so the legend goes, he had thrown an open offer that whosoever succeeded in kidnapping her in a chariot might take her as his bride. The slip was that Oenomaus, an adept in the use of javelins and spears, used to give chase on light chariots pulled by fast horses (Psylla and Harpinna) of high breed given to him by Ares, one of the 12 Olympian gods, and which were the swiftest in Greece. As legend has it, thirteen suitors got away with Hippodemia, but all were invariably caught and promptly transfixed with a royal spear. But then appeared a shrewd young man named Pelops who studied the situation carefully and made sure of his fool-proof arrangements. Now this man Pelops, being such a colourful personality, would bear a more detailed introduction.

He was the son of Tantalus and a grandson of Zeus. Tantalus was on intimate terms with gods and often dined with them. In his pride, he once invited the gods to dine and served them his son Pelops, whom he cut up in pieces and boiled in a cauldron, to test if the gods could recognise human flesh. All the gods, save one, became instantly aware of what was served to them and refused to eat. Only Demeter, who had been lamenting the loss of her daughter Persephone, rather absent-mindedly had a bite at it which incidently happened to be the left shoulder. The gods committed Tantalus to horrible punishment and ordered Hermes to restore Pelops by cooking his flesh in the same cauldron. Rhea later breathed life into the reformed body with an ivory shoulder substituted for the part inadvertently devoured by Demeter. Thus, restored, Pelops assumed such beautiful form and figure that Poseidon felt fascinated and carried him to Mt. Olympus where he fed him on ambrosia.

Pelops, thereafter, returned to his father's kingdom in Paphlagonia but was driven out and landed in Elis as a wanderer where he sued for the hand of Hippodamia.

Even though equipped with winged horses and golden chariot which could skim across the waves, given to him by Poseidon, Pelops made sure of his plan by bribing the King's charioteer, Myrtilus son of Hermes. Myrtilus, who was lured with the promises of half the kingdom and sharing of the bridal night with Hippodemia, removed the lynch pins from the axle of the royal chariot and filled in wax instead. He so camouflaged the replacement that not even Oenomous, who himself used to inspect the chariot before the race, had the ghost of a chance to scent it. The tampering rendered the king's chariot absolutely incapable of bearing the burden of the full blast.

The "smiter of horses" as Homer termed Pelops, left his amiable royal host taking Hippodamia beside him in his chariot for the long course from Pisa, beside the river Alpheus, opposite Olympia, to Poseidon's altar on the Isthmus of Corinth. As usual the royal pursuit followed after a lapse of half an hour during which Oenamaus sacrificed a ram on the alter of Zeus. The pursuit, however, was short-lived and disastrous for Oenamaus as his chariot came down crashing under the thrust of acceleration as soon as the spurious wax pins melted due to the heat caused by friction. The wheels flew off; Oenamaus was suddenly thrown out of his chariot, dragged along and entangled in the reins, met his death instantaneously.

Pelops, Hippodemia and Myrtilus then set out for an evening drive across the sea but when Myrtilus demanded his share of the spoils as per the terms of the conspiracy, Pelops dealt him a sudden kick which sent him flying headlong into the sea at Geraestus, the southernmost tip of Euboea.

Pelops was doubly successful – not only did he earn the bride but also ascended the throne. To herald the acquisition of the empire, he instituted the Olympic games and religious ceremonies on the hallowed ground of Olympia in Elis in 1326 BC. Hippodemia also celebrated the occasion by establishing the Herean games for women.

Unfortunately, the ancient Greek lores and traditions lack the authenticity and fixity of written records. With the passage of time, the Greeks are believed to have amended, improved upon and reconstructed the myths and legends handed down to them in a bid to glorify their past. Even Homer's Iliad and Odyssey are believed to have been reduced to writing long after they were originally composed. HG Wells, in his classic book "The Outline of History", writes : "An early form of Iliad was probably recited by 1000 BC, but it was not written down until perhaps 700 or 600 BC. Many men must have had to do with it as authors and improvers, but later Greek tradition attributed it to a blind bard named Homer, to whom also is ascribed the Odyssey, a composition of a very different spirit and outlook."

With this background, and with the legends as uncertain as they are varied, any attempt to pin-point the exact date or trace the origin of the Olympic Games with any degree of accuracy, will, by and large, be an exercise in futility.

Nevertheless, a study of the early Greek history would equip us with the necessary framework to visualize how, and under what circumstances, the institution of the Olympic Games must have, after all, started.

In the hoary past before the dawn of history (i.e. around 1500 BC) the Greeks were a highly superstitious, wandering race who believed in glorifying human beings. By and large, they were nomads in an excited state, sturdy, undisciplined fighters, much given to consulting Oracles or soothsayers in times of crisis. According to Professor Gilbert Murray, when the oldest man in the tribe could not tell them the right thing to do they went to the Oracles who told them what was the right thing to do or what was the 'will' of the God.

And the soothsayers knew what was healthy and beneficial for the folks then. Greece, owing largely to geographical conditions, dotted with a multitude of valleys, uncommunicable and separated by prong-like arms of mountain ranges, was divided into numerous independent pockets which had failed to coalesce into one; thus, resulting in the birth of warring tribes. Ancient wars being what they were, with man fighting against man face-to-face, the aphorism "survival of the fittest" was more meaningful then than it is in the sophisticated world of today. For their very existence, therefore, the youngmen of Greece had to be sturdy and strong and in the fittest physical state to be available at all times and at a moment's notice to defend their soil. The development of physical strength and skill was, therefore, a must. The Oracles, fully aware of the conditions obtaining, saw in games, sports and physical pursuits a most suitable outlet and a healthy means for toning down the nomadic tendencies of the populace while at the same time keeping alive in them a competitive spirit of keeping fit in a disciplined fashion.

Branded as "The right thing to do or the Will of the God", and coming as it did from the Oracles, the verdict imparted a religious character to the Games. So that the Games came to be treated as most sanctified form of penance for any serious misdeed and symbolic of highest celebrations for any event intended to be glorified. Read in this context, the legends narrated earlier would, perhaps, appear to be nearer the truth.

With so many legends, each pertaining to an entirely different period down the corridor of time, the overall picture seems to be too hazy to decipher, but if we are inclined to give any credence to Pausanias' description in his travelogue we might be reconciled to the conclusion that the beginning of athletic competitions in Olympia dated back to hoary past. There have, however, been interruptions when the games were discontinued but they were subsequently revived from time to time. It is only from 776 BC that the games were religiously held every four years without interruptions for about 1170 years.

Of the earlier games, no records were kept; or, none, at any rate, have come down to us. In fact, in the entire Greek history, there are no recorded events prior to 776 BC. The year 776 BC, i.e., the year of the first recorded Olympic Games, is, therefore, a valuable starting point in Greek chronology whereafter the Greeks started reckoning time by 'Olympiads', the four-year span between the celebrations of the games. Thus, what came to pass after the First Olympiad is history and what lies in antiquity beyond that is myth or mystery.

In the beginning, the ancient authors often cited the name of the Olympic winner of the foot-race for the purposes of dating. Thus, the four-year span between 776 BC and 773 BC was referred to as Coroebus of Elis who was the first victor of the foot-race at the first recorded Olympic Games. Thereafter, with the passage of time and as the number of Olympic champions swelled, the periods of time started to be reckoned in terms of Olympiads.

2

Scene at Olympia

For the better appreciation and more vivid visualisation of the proceedings of the ancient Olympic Games and to understand how the home of one of the great national festivals of Greece looked like in the time of its glory, it would be worthwhile to visualise the image of Olympia, the site of the Olympic Games and its environs. This could not have been possible had it not been for the exploratory works and excavations conducted by the French and the Germans in the nineteenth and twentieth centuries. The pioneering work of excavations on the site of the temple of Zeus is credited to the French Expedition Scientifique de Moree in 1829 which revealed the general plan. Between 1875 and 1881 the Germans, who cherished the project of a complete excavation of Olympia, engaged themselves in large scale diggings and were highly successful in clearing the whole of the sacred precinct, thus fixing the position of the stadium and unearthing the plan of a great Greek sanctuary for the first time. Some small scale exploratory digging was also carried out at the beginning of the twentieth century. This was followed by large-scale efforts by Germans in 1936 which were, however, cut short by the World War II in 1942. In 1952, the work was resumed and by 1960 the stadium, which was buried deep, was fully excavated and restored.

Olympia, after which we call our games, 'The Olympic Games,' by way of paying homage to this masterpiece of the Greek civilisation, is a place in Greece in the western Peloponnese and lies below the heights of Cyllene and Erymanthus. On the northern bank of the river Alpheus (now called Ruphia) about ten miles from its mouth (Longitude: 22^0 East of Greenwich, Latitude : 36^0 North of Equator), Cladeus, a tributary stream merges into the Alpheus just south of Olympia. On the north bank of Alpheus at Olympia there was a wide meadow, a vast stretch of grassy plain; beyond that, arms of low hills covered with luxuriant growth of pine and olive trees dotted with farmlands. Further north, tall and rugged snow-covered peaks obscured the horizon most of the year round.

The Greeks chose the loveliest spot in the land to celebrate the Games and there could be none better than the picturesque meadowland in Olympia where from time immemorial they used to assemble to honour their gods who, they believed, lived on the heights of Mount Olympus.

On this godly spot, the sacred precinct which was also called the Altis or the sacred grove of Zeus was raised. This sacred precinct was in the shape of an irregular quadrangle, about 200 yards long, enclosed by walls on the three sides (west, south and east) with the northern portion gradually ascending and merging with the cavalcadic slopes of the hill of Cronus. Initially, this enclosed area was a place of assemblage for purely religious festivals and so only shrines existed; the principal one being the temple of Hera, the oldest and situated in the north-west portion of the sanctuary. Originally, this was a joint temple of Hera and Zeus and was the most venerable spot in all Greece. In the mid fifth century BC a separate temple of Zeus of even greater dimensions was built. Later on, all kinds of structures, altars, museum, gymnasium, stadium, baths, treasuries, hippodrome, etc., started springing up in and around the sacred precinct.

Encompassed within the Altis, the principal structures, whose remains have been restored as a result of excavations, were the temple of Hera, the temple of Zeus, the Alter of Zeus, the sanctuary of Pelops and the Metroum.

The temple of Zeus was built around 460 BC by Libon, an architect from the neighbouring Elis. This temple housed the giant gold and Ivory statue of Zeus made by an Athenian sculptor named Phidias. It was a most remarkable and impressive statue which finds a place among the seven wonders of the world. Nearly midway between the temples of Hera and Zeus was the open air sanctuary of Pelops in which statues were erected.

Slightly eastwards but almost in the centre of the Altis stood the Altar of Zeus, elliptical in shape with an elevated base approachable by a flight of steps. A mound built with the ash of thighs of those sacrificed to Zeus formed the structure on the base. The total height of the altar was 22 ft. from the ground. The Metroum, which contained statues of the Roman emperors was built in the fourth century BC towards the northernmost part of the Altis and was also known as the temple of the Great Mother of the gods.

Outside the Altis, to the north-west were the Palestra, where wrestlers and boxers trained and marble gymnasium with a covered running track. Towards south-west was Leonidaeum, a large hostel built in fourth century BC meant for the reception of distinguished visitors. The space between the Palestra and the Leonidaeum housed many structures, baths, hospitium, Roman house, Byzantine church, workshop of Phidias, the Athenian sculptor who had made the marvel statue of Zeus.

Towards the north of the Altis there was a set of twelve treasuries in a row which segregated the sacred precinct from the gradual slopes of the hills of Cronus. These treasuries contained the wealth, valuables, offerings, dedicated gifts, etc., made to the sanctuary and are believed to have been built in token of thanks giving and homage to Zeus by the participant states whose competitors gained victories at the Olympics.

In the north-west corner of the Altis was a building named Prytaneum which contained a banquet room meant for ceremonial feasting of the Olympic victors, where the priests and other officials also took their meals. In half the building was the sacred hearth of

Hestia, one of the twelve Olympian gods, on which a fire was kept burning at all times.

Also to the south of the Altis were a number of structures one of them being Bouleuterion or the council house which is relevant to our story. It consisted of two almost identical buildings in an oblong form between which lay a rectangular court in the centre of which rose a statue of Zeus Horkios ('Zeus who presides over Oaths'). Beside this statue, the participants and their families, the trainers and the Judges took a solemn oath before the commencement of the games to keep the competition clean and fair, not to indulge in foul play and to give just decisions.

The main venue of the Games and the centre of throbbing activity during the Olympics was the stadium which lay east of the Altis and which deserves a more elaborate description.

Before the fourth century BC the stadium was nearer to the sacred precinct and almost directly in front of the Altar of Zeus with no walls, etc. cutting it off from the Altis. Later, around the middle of fourth century BC the stadium was shifted about 90 yards (about 82 metres) eastward and a wall Echo Colonnade (so called as the sound echoed seven times or more from it) was built completely segregating it from the sanctuary leaving only a narrow path towards north for entrance.

The main pitch in the stadium where contests were held was about 230 yards long and 35 yards wide. The three sides of the pitch were surrounded by massive sloping embankments made of earth which served as seating accommodation for about 60,000 spectators.

Northwards, the cavalcadic slopes of the hill of Cronus served as natural seating accommodation. An open water channel around the pitch with basins at intervals was made of stone which served as a line of demarcation between the track and the sloping embankments. May be, the water channel served the purpose of deterring spectators from invading or encroaching upon the track or pitch, although knowing how greatly the games were revered, chances of such a sacrilege seem to be remote.

The actual running track started about ten yards away from the end of the western slopes and was marked by a straight line made of stone. A similar line was also marked ten yards from the eastern end of the slope, reducing the entire length of 230 yards of the plain surface to an effective 210 yards (192.27 metres) between the two starting lines. The classic race of this one lap of the stadium was called the 'stade'. The width of the running track sufficed for 20 runners at a time. For the chief judges, called the Hellanodikai, a box made of stone existed on the southern sloping embankment about one-third of the way from the starting line near the Altis. Just opposite to this box, that is on the slopes of the Cronus hill, was an altar of Demeter Chamyne from which the priests of the cult watched the games.

The stadium was connected with the sacred precinct with a narrow passage towards north which was called Krypte or covered entrance and through which the athletes and the judges entered the stadium. Just before this narrow entrance there was a row of some sixteen bronze statues of Zeus built out of fines imposed on erring or defaulting athletes who, in one way or the other, infringed the rules of the games or were guilty of indulging in foul play. These statues called 'Zanes' reminded the athletes just before entry into the main arena to observe strict discipline and to be fair during the games.

3

Olympic Regimen in Ancient Times

The games were held at the time of the full Moon in the month of Apollonius or Parthenius, i.e. on the day of the first full moon after the summer solstice, — a time of the year which almost synchronises with the month of August of the present era.

The Olympic festival was pentaeteris, i.e. according to the ancient mode of reckoning, a space of four years elapsed between each festival. More precisely, they were held alternately at intervals of 49 to 50 lunar months (lunar year being shorter than the solar, such an adjustment was necessary to keep date with the summer solstice). Thus, in the former case the festival fell in the month of Apollonius and in the latter in the month of Parthenius – both names of Elean or Olympian months.

At first the games were confined to only one day and the programme consisted of only one event, the foot-race of one length of the stadium, the race of one stade which was called 'Dromos'. This lone event programme continued for 13 Olympics but in the 14th Olympics another race of two stades, called the 'Diaulos' was added, which required the athletes to run the stade and then back again around a post. In the 15th a long distance race of 24 lengths (about $2^{2/3}$ miles) was added, which was called 'Dolichos'. This race was won by Ladas, hailing from Sparta, who collapsed and died at the finish to become the first posthumous winner of an Olympic event.

The 18th Olympics held in 708 BC marked the introduction of Pentathlon consisting of five events— broad jump, javelin throw, one stade, discus throw and wrestling. (Wrestling, which made its appearance thus in the Olympics, later became a separate event). Boxing was added at the 23rd Olympics: the 25th games saw the advent of equestrian events and in the 33rd Olympics was added a very manly but savage item, called Pankration, which combined wrestling and boxing in one. In 520 BC, a race of two stades was initiated in which the participants had to run bare with heavy round shields and plumed helmets. This race was known as 'hoplite' and was the last among the important additions to the games.

The events in the Olympic games continued to multiply and with contests for boys also added, the duration of the games from the lone morning show in the beginning was naturally extended to five days including two days exclusively meant for religious ceremonies.

In the fifth century BC, the programme during the five days of actual Olympic meet used to be as follows:

The first day was reserved for initiatory sacrifices and for scrutinizing the eligibility of the contestants when all the competitors were classed and arranged by the judges. After the oath taking ceremony which was held in the Bouleuterion, also called the Council House, contests between the trumpeteers took place and to this succeeded on the same day and the next the contests for boys. On the second day, chariot and horse races and the pentathlon events were gone through. Sacrifices of a pig to Zeus and a black ram to Pelops were offered on the third day, which appears to have been the principal one, and on the afternoon of the same day the main athletic events for men were gone through. On the morning of the fourth day the left-over athletic events were continued while in the afternoon competitions in wrestling, boxing and pankration events used to be held; in all, there used to be 24 events on card — 18 for men and 6 for boys. It may be noted in passing that 24 events were the maximum to have been held in any one ancient Olympic games. The fifth and the final day was wholly devoted to processions and sacrifices, feasting, rejoicings and to the banquets given by the Eleans to the victors in the games.

By the 77th games, the programme had become so much crowded that the events, per force, used to be gone through till late in the night. Callias, an Athenian boxer, is known to have protested that due to late chariot races he was made to fight in moonlight.

The games were held under the strict superintendence of judges, called the Hellanodikai, who were chosen by lot from the whole body of Eleans. The judges were instructed for ten months in the gymnasia before they qualifed to conduct the games. They were obliged solemnly to swear that they would be absolutely impartial in their judgement. In the discharge of their duties and in keeping order and maintaining discipline they were assisted by certain officers called 'alutai', similar to the Roman Lictors.

In all, ten judges used to preside over the games. But if Pausanias' account is to be accepted, the number of judges varied quite often. According to him, at first there were only two judges but in the 75th Olympics nine judges were appointed, three of whom had the superintendence of the horse races, three of the Pentatholon and three of the remaining contests. Two Olympiads after, a tenth judge was added. In the 103rd Olympics, the number was increased to twelve as at that time there were twelve Elean Phylae and a judge was chosen from each tribe. But as the Eleans afterwards lost part of their lands in war with the Arcadians, the number of Phylae was reduced to eight in the 104th Olympiad and accordingly there were then only eight judges. But in the 108th Olympic games the number of judges was increased to ten and remained the same in the time of Pausanias.

Participation in the games was at first restricted to free born Greek citizens only having a clean past record and who were not more than 35 years in age. This was when Greece was clustered with small city-states. But later, with the establishment of empires, the games attracted atheletes from the Macedonian world and Roman empire.

The first Olympic victor in the first recorded Olympic games in 776 BC was Croebus – who won the foot-race of one stade. As winner he was crowned with a wreath of wild olive symbolising the highest award conceived in Greece then.

Olive (Oles europaea) is one of the worlds oldest cultivated crops. In Homer's times annointing the body with olive oil was considered to be a highly prised luxury. Olive has from time immemorial, been held in high reverence and considered a symbol of peace and sanctity. The Old Testament speaks of an olive leaf that the dove brought back to the Noah's ark. According to the ancient poets, Hercules considered the planting of an olive tree brought from the lands of Hyperboreans in the sacred grove north of the temple of Zeus in Olympia a great religious performance.

Even earlier than that a Greek legend has it that in a contest between Poseidon and Athena for possession of the city of Athens, Poseidon struck the rock of the Acropolis with his trident and a well of salt water gushed forth. Athena, on the other hand, planted an olive tree beside the well and as this was considered the highest and most sacred gift, Athena was awarded the city which speaks of the reverence and esteem in which any act connected with olive was held in ancient Greece.

The only prize with which the winner used to be honoured was a garland of wild olive which according to the Elean legends, was the prize originally instituted by the Idaean Heracles. This tradition was scrupulously followed when the games were subsequently revived by the more famous Heracles when he decreed that the victors in the contests should be crowned with Olive leaves only as he himself had not received payment for his labours for Eurystheus. The olive wreaths were cut from the Kallistephanos – the sacred tree of Heracles – which according to legends and Pindar, had been brought by him from Ister (an ancient name for river Danube) in the north, also called the land of Hyperboreans, and planted in the sacred grove at Altis. Such small and trifling an award was believed to stimulate courage and virtue.

This practice, however, appears to have lost favour in later times when the games were revived by Iphitus. The prizes then possessed some intrinsic value of which tripods were a common variety. This practice appears to have continued till 756 BC but from the seventh Olympiad, with the approbation of the oracle at Delphi, the crown of wild olive was substituted and became the sole reward of the victors.

Originally, the victor, who was styled Olympionikai, used to be crowned upon a tripod made of, or covered with, bronze but afterwards upon a table made of ivory and gold by Colotes, a pupil and collaborator of Phidias. This was the practice in vogue at least till the second century AD as evidenced by Pausansias himself. The name of the victor and that of his father and of his country were then proclaimed by a herald before the representatives of the assembled Greeks.

The victor on return rode in a chariot drawn by four white horses to the temple of the most important god of his home area and deposited his victor's wreath on the altar as an offering to the god.

The ancient Greeks were great connoisseurs and admirers of the perfectly developed human physique. For them there was no better spectacle than a perfectly built, symmetrical human body. This is amply reflected in the countless master pieces of Greek architecture.

The awareness of the beauty of naked human forms raised them to heights of ecstasy. No wonder, therefore, that the Greek religion instinctively became associated with, and centred round the worship of an ideally developed human figure. And since the attainment of a perfect physical form was considered possible only through strict discipline and healthy physical pursuits, the games which required both these in abundant measure, also came to be regarded as religious obligations. The athletic demonstrations and religious observances were, therefore, so much superimposed and intermingled so closely that it is not possible to distinguish one from the other and to guess where one ended and the other began.

For these physical and religious reasons, therefore, we hear of varied and numerous athletic festivals which were in vogue in ancient Greece. Besides, the Olympic Games, which form the theme of our story, there were the Pythian, Isthmian, Nemean, Herean and so many other games.

The Pythian Games, which were only next in importance to the Olympic Games used to be held at Delphi in honour of Apollo every four year (Pythiad) beginning in the third year of an Olympiad. Originally the Pythian Games were held every eight years but from 582 BC they became quadrennial and Panhellenic. The Pythian Games are believed to have been first celebrated by Adrastus King of Argos in 1263 BC.

The Isthmian Games were biennial and used to be held about April-May in the second and fourth years of every Olympiad in honour of god Poseidon.

The Nemean Games were held in honour of Zeus in the Valley of Nemea near Phlius in the Argolid. They were also biennial, being held around July in the same years as the Insthmian Games.

The Herean Games, called Heraea, were held in honour of Hera and were established by Hippodemia to celebrate her marriage with Pelops. (The story has already been detailed in the first chapter). The games were confined to Elean virgins and were presided over by a board of matrons. They used to be held immediately after the Olympic Games.

There are also traditions of games celebrated at Elis in very early times: and Hesiod, who is supposed to have been a contemporary of Homer, refers to games at Chalicis, wherein he gained a prize for song.

These and numerous other athletic festivals were the order of the day in ancient Greece but any detailed description of any of these is outside the scope of this work.

The games were virtually sanctified and treated at the highest moral and religious plane. No one with a suspect police record, or even related to any such person, was allowed to participate. Among the unrelaxable qualifications were strict amateurism and absolute faith in the gods. Preparations for participation in the games were started one year in advance when preliminary contests were held in different city-states and the pick of the qualifiers were required to undergo rigorous training for ten months under the watchful eyes of coaches and expert trainers. Only those qualifiers who could undergo such strenuous and rigorous preliminary training schedule were allowed to journey to Olympia where they were further required to observe a stricter regimen for another month at the gymnasium situated north-west outside of the sacred precinct of Altis. The Gymnasia were special buildings provided by the state and managed by public officials.

The training under the supervision of trainers and judges started early in the morning and continued till late in the evening. The diet during this training period was strictly regulated and light. For breakfast, only fermented bread and grape juice were served. Lunches were skipped to keep away lethargy so that there may be no let-up in punishing exercises throughout the day. A somewhat substantial dinner was allowed; in earlier Olympics it consisted only of fruits, vegetables and plenty of cheese. Fish and meat were later additions to the menu. Alcoholic beverages and cold drinks were prohibited. Strict observance and adherence to discipline was the keynote of the training programme and the judges did not hesitate to use sticks and canes to enforce discipline.

The first ritual before the commencement of the games was the assembly of athletes, trainers and judges before the statue of God Zeus in the sacred precinct to pay homage. On the solemn occasion, they took a solemn oath on slices of boars flesh in the name of the god to observe the rules, to be fair and honest in their actions and turnouts during the games. The athletes took an additional oath that they had spent at least ten months in preparation for the games and that they would observe only fair means in attempting to win their contests. Everyone also prayed for his personal success as well as the success of the games. Then they proceeded towards the stadium under the shadows of the Zanes which were once again a reminder to them for strict observance of rules.

The athletes, city-wise and state-wise, marched around the stadium in a ceremonial parade and were then ready for the contests that followed. The start and finish of each contest was heralded with the blowing of trumpets.

The preparations, conduct and the esteem and honour accorded to the victors of the Olympic Games were all witnessed in a manner which smacked of a religious fervour. The holy month in which the games were held was called 'Hieromenia', derived from *hieroi* meaning sacred, (which fell at intervals of alternately 49 and 50 lunar months, i.e., four calendar years) during which all hostilities were suspended and sacred truce (ekecheiria) was proclaimed prohibiting all violence.

Some time before the games, delegates called Spondophoroi used to be sent throughout Greece to announce the commencement of the festival — proclamation which meant that the sacred truce was operative from thence onwards till the completion of the games. Breach of the sacred truce was considered a sacrilege. Athletes and spectators both were believed to enjoy the traditional protection of the watchful eyes of the gods during their journeys to and from the sacred Olympia. Arms and weapons were prohibited inside the sacred precinct. The city-states and small principalities which were constantly at war with each other considered it a religious obligation to call it a day and cease the hostilities to enable peaceful conduct of the games. The swords were sheathed during even the famous battles of Thermopylae and Salamis in 480 BC, the first year of the 75th Olympiad, and while the state itself was in mortal peril, a vast multitude cheered the finalists of the boxing event in which Theagenes, the great and Euthymus participated.

On one occasion when the Spartans found themselves tempted to ignore the sacred truce and marched against the fortress of Phyreum and Lepreum, they were fined by the Eleans 2,000 minae, being two for each hoplite (an armed soldier).

In 420 BC, all the Lacedaemonians were debarred from participating in the 90th Olympic Games because they had not paid the fine imposed on them for violating the Elean territory during the sacred truce.

4

Heroes of Ancient Olympics

Unique were the laurels and honours showered upon an Olympic victor. At once he became a national hero, an idol, a person extolled to the skies and sung as a deity. Sculptors carved his statues for display and in remembrance of the feat for posterity.

Phidias (son of Charmides), an immortal name among the ancient Greek sculptors, who had his own workshop towards the west of the Altis and who had chiseled the marble statue of Zeus was among the numerous sculptors who immortalised many an Olympic victor in stone. Poets of the eminence of Simonides, Euripides and Pindar composed odes and paeans of praise. Nearly four complete books of such odes written by the famous poet Pindar have survived which rank in the forefront of the greatest lyrics in Greek literature. Less known, but still of a very high order, are the poems by Bacchylides.

On the victor's triumphant return to his native city a special opening was made in the boundary walls for his entry which was symbolic of the highest honour and respect paid to him. The idea behind this symbolic gesture, presumably, was that when such a strongman lived in the city there was no necessity of any protective wall. The entire population of the city turned out to receive and paraded around to accord a tumultuous welcome to the homecoming hero. Exaenetus, on his return to his city of Agrigentum, after winning a foot-race at one of the Olympics, is known to have been driven around in a four-horse chariot piloted by a fleet of no less than 300 dignitaries, each in his own chariot pulled by a couple of pedigree horses.

Hearty and warm reception was an undisputed privilege of an Olympic champion. There runs the story of Oebotas of Achaia, who won the foot race at the sixth Olympics in 756 BC. He considered his homecoming celebrations not upto his expectations and in the result cursed the town in disgust. Curiously enough, for 296 years thereafter, the town of Achaiya could not produce a single Olympic winner. The advice of the Oracle of Delphi was sought on whose bidding a statue of Oebotas was raised long after his death. At the very next Olympics, Sostratas of Achais won the foot-race in the boys events.

Besides such honours, an Olympic victor of the ancient games virtually earned for himself a life-long social security. He was exempted from the payment of all direct or indirect taxes; hotel owners offered him free food and drinks for life; physicians administered free medical aid; barbers gave free hair cuts, masseurs free massages; damsels vied with each other for his hand and so forth. In fact, he could have anything for the asking and if he intended to participate in the next Olympics, he was assured of all the expenses for preparations.

By and large, the events in the ancient Olympic Games were held more or less in the same fashion as they are today. But there were some major variations, too. For instance, the athletes performed in complete nudity, keeping exposed the beauty of their frame. Even for long distance races there were no elliptical tracks; instead, all races were run flat and the athletes were required to run to and fro turning around a flag post to make up the distance. In long jumps, the contestants carried weights (called halteres, a kind of dumbbell) in their hands which they flung backwards while taking off. The classification of contestants was by age alone: boys, adolescents and men as against heavyweight, lightweight etc., of today. In chariot races, it was the owner of the chariot and not the charioteer, who won the prize. Similarly, in the equestrian events it was the owner of the horses who was honoured.

In wrestling, which according to Plutarch, was the most artistic event of the games, the wrestlers, after smearing themselves with olive oil, which rendered their bodies slippery, used to sprinkle dust over themselves to allow the opponent a firm grip. Only clean falls counted, and that too, when the winner continued to be on his feet while his opponent was down on the ground. In boxing, the contestants protected their hands with himantes – long straps of soft leather wound around the fists.

Perhaps the most exacting and the one which required an allround superb skill was the pentathlon event. Even the great philosopher, Aristotle, appreciated the high qualities and the general built-up that were the pre-requisites for pentathlon champion. Although, it comprised half the number of events of the decathlon of today, its mode of conduct had made it most difficult, and at the same time most coveted. It was, in essence, an elimination contest wherein the field of the contestants narrowed down as the event progressed. It started with the broad jump and all those who leapt a prescribed distance qualified for the javelin throw. Only the first four in the javelin throw forged ahead for the third item – the one foot-race. In this race only the one who finished last was eliminated and the first three who covered the distance quickest, tried their hands at the discus throw. The first two who out did the third in heaving the 12-pound discuss the farthest qualified for the final which was the great wrestling match fought to the finish.

The ultimate winner in wrestling was the one who gained first three falls over his opponent. Mere pinning the opponent's shoulder to the ground did not count a fall, however. He had to be grounded while the winner was still on his feet.

If the pentathlon event was the most exacting and demanded supreme all round skill and stamina, the pankration was the most brutal and barbaric. It was a combination of boxing and wrestling in which all types of holds, punches, fists, twists etc. were allowed. In fact, except biting and pinching the eyes, all and every conceivable strangleholds applied to force the opponent into submission were permitted. That being so, a winner emerged only when his opponent, unable to bear the torture any further, raised his hand in token of surrender.

A pankration champion, therefore, had to be extremely robust and rugged with a lot of courage and ability to withstand excruciating pain and torture. Such was the brutal savagery attending this contest that the famed Arrachion of Phingalia lay dead while he was being declared the winner. During the final of the pankration event Arrachion found himself on the receiving end when his opponent clamped a stranglehold as a result of which he began to lose consciousness. Still unyielding and with the champion like never-say-die determination, Arrachion started twisting the rival's foot out of sockets with a force and rigidity which was taking the toll of his own life. The opponent writhing in agony and unable to sustain any further torture raised his hand slowly. The referees rushed to separate the two and declared Arrachion the winner, who alas, was by then no more.

The brute force the pankration champions possessed and the torture that they were capable of inflicting on their opponents is amply reflected in the feats credited to Polydamas of Thessaly. Polydamas is known to have killed a lion all by himself, halted a chariot drawn by horses at full gallop by simply holding the rear portion of the chariot with one hand, and subdued a wild bull running berserk by simply holding firmly one of his hind legs. Again in a simultaneous fight against three men, he killed all of them. Unfortunately, however, what was Polydamas' strong point ultimately proved his doom. He met his death in a cave when instead of fleeing to safety he, confident of his prowess, tried to save the roof from caving and was crushed under the debris.

Another name that is taken in the same breath is Theagenes, son of Timosthenes (a priest of Hercules) hailing from Thasos. He is known to have possessed almost superhuman strength even while he was running in the tiny-tots category. He could transport life-size statues all by himself with comfortable ease. To think of his performance while he had seen no more than nine summers...!

In his career that spanned well over two decades he accomplished an all time record of bagging about 1,400 championships in the three events that he was the complete master: races, boxing and pankration.

Theagenes was essentially a pankration specialist but in the 75th Olympics in 480 BC he entered in the boxing event as well. In the final he met Euthymus, another boxer of repute who was much senior and had been Olympic champion in the past.

Theagenes did win the boxing title but was so severely baffled and battered in the bout that he had per force to stay out of the pankration final in which also he had qualified. This default on the part of Theagenes which deprived Euthymus of a title and afforded a walkover victory to the other pankration finalist was viewed with serious displeasure by the judges who charged Theagenes with greediness and an attempt to bite more than he could chew. He was fined, which he paid and did not compete in boxing in the following Olympics (76th) enabling Euthymus to have an easy sailing. In the 77th Olympics, however, Theagenes contested both the pankration and boxing events and had the unique distinction of winning in both.

Notwithstanding his temporary disgrace, the townsmen of Thasos raised Theagenes a statue. Meanwhile, the heart of Euthymus was burning with jealousy against him. The aggrieved rival, therefore, stole in the dead of night and cut the base of the statue in a bid to topple it down. The statue did topple with a vengeance; it tumbled right over the marauding rival resulting in his instantaneous death.

Such was the fame of Theagenes' prowess that the people believed he could deal a blow even in absentia.

Going by the records that have survived, however, the pride of place undoubtedly would go to Glaucus of Arthedon, the all-time boxing champion. The Olympic records are replete with the feats performed by his mailed fists.

Then there was Milo of Croton, a giant among wrestlers, who won six consecutive wrestling crowns at the Olympics during the sixth century BC Milo's strength, stamina and skills were fabulous. During his career, which spread over nearly three decades, he reigned supreme and not only did he never know the word defeat but his knees also never touched the ground during innumerable encounters. Besides, he had elements of showmanship and plenty of tricks up his sleeves with which he was prone to entertain the crowds by exhibition of his strength par excellence. Stories of his showmanship, which have withstood the onslaughts of time, include holding of a pomegranate in his hand with such a firm grip that even the concerted efforts of several strongmen together could not dislodge it. And at the same time his hold over it was so controlled and contrived that the fruit was not crushed under the impact. Milo took delight in positioning himself on a disc, rendered slippery with profuse application of oil and grease, and then challenging the strongmen to dislodge him. Single handedly he thwarted the attempts of several of them at a time and with an air of triumph stepped down when the challengers badly bruised, retreated in shame. And then to show what super-human muscular strength he possessed even in the parts where muscles as such do not exist, he would tie a cord round his head and snap it by swelling the veins and arteries.

Milo was believed to have acquired such fabulous strength by his practice of carrying a calf on his shoulders daily and continuing the exercise even after the calf had grown into a full grown bull.

Judged by any standards and of any period he was a physical prodigy, indeed. Likewise, he had a phenomenal appetite, too. The quantities he is believed to have devoured in single sittings baulk the imagination: eight kilos of meat and bread washed down with over a gallon of wine.

Like Polydamas, however, the abundance of bodily strength and the over-confidence in his own prowess ultimately brought about Milo's end in tragic circumstances. Passing through a jungle all alone, he noticed a woodcutter's job only partially done with a wedge fixed in the thick stem of a tree. He thought that by felling the tree he could give a pleasant surprise to the woodcutter on his return. Substituting his hand for the woodcutter's axe he whacked with such force that the wedge gave way and Milo's hand got entrapped in the stem beyond retrieve. Thus, stuck up, the flesh in him was ready feast for the pack of wild wolves and the woodcutter on return saw the ghastly sight of a human skeleton instead of a felled tree.

Numerous such names and stories of their fantastic strength and feats may be traced from the ancient games. Dwelling on them further will neither enhance the glory nor their omission belittle the traditions of that golden age of Greece.

The games were well attended with nearly 40,000 to 60,000 spectators jampacking the slopes on the four sides of the stadium. But women were not allowed presumably because the contestants were required to perform in complete nudity. Women were not even allowed to cross the river Alpheus during the games. The solitary exception, however, was the priestess of Demeter Chamyne for whom a special seat used to be reserved on the slopes of the hills of Cronus. Penalty for female trespassers was certain death by being hurtled down from a nearby cliff named Mount Typaeum.

An uproarious situation, however, once arose when Pisidores won the boxing championship. His mother, Pherenice (or Callipatria) of Rhodes, having seen through Pisidores' training on his father's death, could not resist the temptation of being in the midst while her son performed. Her son's victory proved too much for her restraint and she leapt to the middle, shedding in the process the disguise she had put on and thus exposing her sex. A compassionate view was, however, taken in her case because of her rich heritage and the high sporting traditions to which she belonged – she was the daughter of Diagoras, an Olympic champion, and her brothers, too, had distinguished themselves at the games. Thenceforth, to avoid such a recurrence, the trainers were also required to appear in complete nudity.

Subsequently, after considerable passage of time, rules were relaxed and women were allowed as spectators. Women were, however, allowed to send chariots to the races and the first woman whose horses won the prize was Cynisca, the daughter of Archidamus and sister of Agesilaus. Later on, they were even allowed to participate and at the 128th Olympics in 268 BC, Belisiche, a woman from Macedonia, drove a pair of colts to win the chariot race.

5

Games Suspended

It was due entirely to the religious sanctity attached to the games, their lofty ideals and the solid foundations on which the edifice of Olympic movement was built by the Greeks that this healthy and exalted institution continued uninterrupted for well over eleven centuries. In fact, few, if any, man-made endeavours have lasted so long in the annals of mankind. So it is all the more poignant that such a noble institution should have come to such an unceremonious end in 393 AD when the Roman Emperor Theodosius I (373 – 395 AD) peremptorily suspended the games by a decree branding it a pagan festival and a public nuisance. Theodosius had embraced Christianity and would no longer tolerate sacrifices or other such celebrations.

The circumstances leading to, and culminating into the ignominious exit of the ancient Olympic games are traceable to the degradation that had crept in centuries earlier. And then, most ironically, indeed, it was the pinnacle of success and the height of reverence that the institution of games had acquired which ultimately became the root cause of its unceremonious end.

It all started over the dispute as to who were the real custodians with the privilege of conducting the biggest show on earth. The rivalry between the Elians and the Pisates in this regard had its roots in the hoary past.

The management and control of the sacred precinct in Olympia rested with the neighbouring town of Pisa with Elis having a minor share in it. The Elians, however, had more sporting traditions to boast about and they were, therefore, the de facto organisers of the earliest games. The judges (Hellanodikal) used to be all Elians who were known for their high morals and fair play. In 748 BC, however, the Pisates, with the backing of King Pheidon of Arogos, attempted to usurp this privilege whereupon the Elians sought the help of Sparta and managed to retain the control. The issue seemed to have been finally resolved in 570 BC when the Elians inflicted a crushing defeat on Pisa; but the Pisates did not lose heart and in fourth century BC once more showed up to preside over the games. The Elians who considered it an usurpation and an unwarranted intrusion upon their birth right did not hesitate to invade the sanctuary while the 104th Olympic Games were in progress and forced the Pisates to take to their heels.

Whatever might be the merits of the case, ekecheiria, the sacred truce, whose breach was considered to be a sacrilege, was, at any rate, violated.

And then there were the destructive tendencies emanating from human frailties, selfishness, greed, lust for personal laurels and the dubious and questionable means to achieve them. A win at the Olympic games was rated as the highest honour one could achieve. Even the kings and other high dignitaries vied for one. The code of strict amateurism, which was the keynote of Olympic ideals, therefore, began to be violated more non-challantly than ever before and the spirit behind it thrown to the four winds. The inviolate sanctity hitherto attached to the games was flagrantly set at naught and the rules followed more in breach than in observance. All this, in a nutshell, to gain a victory at the Olympics by hook or crook, by fair means or foul.

The canker had set in even while the Greeks were in command. The decadence was amply reflected in their architecture and sculpture too. From the mid fourth century BC, the athletic male figures no longer predominated; instead, wanton and vulgar images and poses of female figures emerged from the chisel. The phenomenon of vulgarity made its appearance more markedly.

In the second century BC when the Romans conquered Greece, they carried away masterpieces of the earlier Greek sculpture and with it vanished whatever little was left of the highest and the noblest traditions.

In the result, the games bereft of the high plane on which they were conducted and with the Romans dominating the scenario, were reduced to an irredeemable farce. The high moral and sacred values became extinct. Bribery, corruption and malpractices became rampant. Professionalism, in sharp contrast to strict amateurism, became the order of the day. The manner in which Nero participated in the games is an indication, if any was needed, of the lowest depth the games had struck.

Nero Claudius Ceasar (AD 37-68), the Roman emperor who ruled from AD 54 to AD 68 and who is known for his tyranny and murder of his own mother and wife, was also to a great extent, responsible for the slow but certain murder of the ancient Olympic Games. In 67 AD he visited Olympia with a retinue of about 5000 strong to applaud him on winning Olympic laurels. It is worth while to note that the year 67 AD was not an Olympic year and hence no games were scheduled to be held. But Nero literally 'summoned' the Olympic Games to sychronise with his visit to Greece, which was simply a province of his imperial domain and therefore, whatever he did had the sanction of whosoever that mattered. He built a house to the east of the 'hippodrome' and styled it the 'House of Nero'. All the other competitors were either forced to withdraw from the events in which he participated or were bribed to stay out. The field thus cleared, the championship for him was assured.

In the chariot race, pulled by ten horses, he faltered and stumbled but was assisted by the judges, to regain his feet and then declared the winner. In all the other events that he competed, various chariot races, singing and playing musical instruments, he declared himself the winner. Of course, he was the judge, jury and competitor, all in one.

The fact that the games survived and lingered for another two centuries did not signify that they were any the popular; it was simply indicative of the solid foundations on which the games were laid, which required centuries to demolish.

The sanctuary sustained several onslaughts and, as a result of repeated attacks coupled with the furies of nature, the Olympia, and with it, its name and fame, got buried fathoms deep as if hiding its face in shame.

In 267 AD, it was severely damaged by the invasion of Hiruli. This damage was, however, partially repaired by building fortification walls around shrines by using the debris of the ruins. In 393 AD, at the instance of Alaria, the Goths from north plundered the sacred precinct. About 33 years later, in 426 AD, Theodosius II got the boundary walls around the Altis razed to the ground. As if all this was not enough, severe earthquakes, a century later, destroyed whatever little remained and the rivers Alpheus and Cladius dramatically changed their course as if to make sure that the last remnants did not leave a trace behind. In retrospect, however, a novel way to put it would be to say that the two rivers did a signal service to posterity by protecting from further ravages of whatever had remained by covering them with hundreds of feet of silt and thus preserving the ruins.

The last recorded name in the row of Olympic champions is that of Varastades, an Armenian prince who won the boxing title.

Varastades later became the king of Armenia but it is not because of his royal status that he is remembered in the realm of Olympics. But just as Coroebus' name is spelt in the context of ancient Olympics being the first ever recorded winner, Varasdates was the last in the line.

6

Games Revived

To say that Baron Pierre de Coubertin was the chief motivating force in resurrecting the Olympic movement in the present era would be the bare truth, though not the whole of it and also not exactly either. Nevertheless, he can aptly be called the Father of the Modern Olympic Games.

Other persons who were responsible for the revival in no small measure also deserve special citation in the same breath, about them a bit later.

Coubertin was born in Paris on January 1, 1863. His family had earmarked military career for him and accordingly he was sent for education to St. Cyr., the renowned French Military Academy. Coubertin, however, had his own ideas about his future and he thought he might more profitably channelise his talents and energy towards improving the lot of the younger generation of France through competitive sports and thereby strengthen the nation. Accordingly, he abandoned the military career and set about his own chosen task earnestly.

The galling memories of the humiliating defeat inflicted by the Germans in the Franco Prussain war of 1870 still haunted the Frenchmen. Coubertin ascribed the low morals and the moral degradation of his countrymen to something radically wrong in the upbringing of the youths at the college and university stages.

He was a widely travelled man and had noticed with concern that compared to the youths of the United States and Britain, where sports was an integral part of education, the activities of competitive sports and games were sadly lacking in the curricula of French youths due mainly to the prevalent notion in France that athletic pursuits were detrimental to the advancement of education. But on his part, Coubertin was firmly convinced that healthy competitions constituted the essential ingredients of the development of the high qualities of character, courage and physical fitness. Being so obsessed, he resigned his commission, studied political science and engaged himself in studying and analysing the problems of education – national and international.

Meanwhile, Olympia and with it the grandeur of the ancient Olympic Games, after lying buried for centuries, was, once again, in full view as a result of six years (1875 – 1881) of extensive excavations by the Germans and was attracting tourists from far and near. Coubertin was one of them and while on the scene, the majestic ruins seem to have forcefully reminded him of the glory of the Olympic Games and the exploits and feats performed there in the hoary past. The notion struck the baron why it should not be possible to revive the lost glory of the Olympics and once again unite the diverse peoples of the world through sports on a common platform. Fired by missionary zeal he set about the task in right earnest and dedicated the rest of his life and fortune towards achieving this goal.

Coubertin was a great acamedician and a prolific writer. His Universal History in four volumes is a remarkable work as also his "Memoires Olympiques" considered as the finest history of the games available. During the better part of his life, Olympics was the central theme of his writings. "Olympia and the Olympics symbolise an entire civilisation superior to countries, cities, military heroes or even the ancient religions."

On relinquishing the presidency of the International Olympic Committee in 1925 he rounded up his philosophic recollections thus: "Despite a certain amount of disillusion which for a time dashed my finest hopes I believe in the moral and peaceful virtues of sports.

On the playing fields men are no longer political or social friends or enemies, but only fellow players playing the same game."

It was late in 1892 at a meeting of the Athletic Sports Union in Paris that Coubertin for the first time publicly propounded the idea of reviving the Olympic Games. He appealed to the assembly: "Let us export oarsmen, runners, fencers; this is the free trade of the future – and on the day when it shall take its place among the customs of Europe, the cause of peace will have received a new and powerful support. So please help me re-establish the Olympic Games."

His appeal received a lukewarm response and polite applause as the audience considered his proposals too Utopian to be practicable. But the short statured baron (he stood only 5 feet 3 inches) was not the one to lose heart and he clung to his project with a missionary zeal.

On June 16, 1894, Coubertin presented an exhaustive and comprehensive plan for the revival of the Olympic Games before the Congress which was attended by representatives of the USA, USSR, UK, Sweden, Spain, Greece, Italy and Belgium, besides other dignitaries, notable among them being the Duke of Sparta, the Prince of Wales, the King of Belgium and the Crown Prince of Sweden.

Coubertin was so successful in firing the imagination of his audience that on 23rd of the same month the Congress unanimously approved in principle the revival of the Olympic Games. The tiny Baron's life dream had come true. The move at once got such an enthusiastic and spontaneous response and support that not only was the venue agreed upon but the year 1900 – more convenient for a start of the Olympics – was considered too long a wait; instead, it was advanced by four years to be held in 1896.

The delegates would have very much preferred Olympia itself as the venue but the site there was absolutely unfit for the purpose and was beyond reconstruction and restoration.

From the events narrated so far an impression might have been created that Coubertin was the first to try for the revival of the Olympic Games. But the fact of the matter is that whilst several others tried and failed and were therefore forgotten, Coubertin was lucky enough to have succeeded.

In fact, it were the Greeks themselves who first made any concrete effort in this direction. Nearly four years before Coubertin was born, a wealthy Greek living in Rumania, Evangelios Zappas, placed his entire fortune at the disposal of the Greek government for restoring the Olympic glory.

The Greek government readily accepted the generous offer and during the 30 years period from 1859 attempted four times to organise the games in Greece – first on November 15, 1859 followed by attempts on November 15, 1870, May 18, 1875 and May 18, 1889. Unfortunately, all of them ended in big flops due to lack of foresight and organisational ability.

In the absence of any stadium, the games of 1859, were held in an improvised locale and on the streets of Athens. It turned out to be an utter mockery of the games. The presence of the king and the queens notwithstanding, chaos and confusion ruled the proceedings. To gain vantage positions and to get past the police cordon every Tom, Dick and Harry, even invalid and disabled persons pretended to be competitors. In the melee that followed, many were injured and the programme was somehow willy – nilly gone through. It is purely for academic interest to recall that nine events were gone through on that occasion. They were : 200 metres, 400 metres and 1,500 metres runs, discus and javelin throws, long jump, two specialised jumps involving ditches and leather bags and climbing. In the subsequent attempts, some more events were added but they would not bear recounting as they do not have any bearing on our story.

The remaining three efforts hardly showed anything to merit mention except that they were held in the ancient stadium of Athens which had by then been renovated. Nevertheless, the enthusiasm, will and determination to revive the centuries old glory was more than manifest and it will be only appropriate to say that between the ancient and the modern Olympic Games these abortive, yet well-intentioned attempts formed a valuable link.

7

The Teething Troubles

The 1896 games in Athens were a splendid success. The dreams of Zappas and Coubertine had come true and the Olympic movement was once again firmly established. The fare was well publicised; the enthusiasm was at fever pitch even though the performances were below expectations as it more than fulfilled the ideal Coubertine had envisioned, i.e., uniting the youths of the world on a common platform. Besides, it was fully in harmony with the Olympic Creed the Baron had coined : 'The important thing in the Olympic Games is not winning but taking part. The essential thing in life is not conquering but fighting well.'

Despite the promising start, however, an under current of trouble was simmering. Egged by narrow parochial considerations the Greek government and the Zappas brothers felt sore over the dominance of Coubertin and the International Olympic Committee in the organisation of the Games which they thought was their exclusive domain. Their line of thinking was that had it not been for the huge funds donated by Zappas Averoof, the Greek government and money raised by Crown Prince Constantine the games would not have seen the light of the day. And on top of it they wanted Athens to be the permanent venue of all future Olympics. The demand was put forth in no uncertain terms by King George I of Greece. 'May Greece be destined to become the peaceful meeting ground of all nationalities, and may Athens become the permanent seat of the Olympic Games'.

Besides, the Greeks in general had another grouse – the athletes from the United States had made clean sweep of almost all the events. This had deeply hurt their vanity.

Coubertin, on the other hand was implacably firm in imparting an international character to the games in keeping with the resolution adopted at the International Congress in 1894 that the games would be held in different cities of the world by rotation.

Fortunately, two factors averted an open cleavage among the big wigs of the Olympic Games and thereby saved the games from jeopardy. First, Greece entangled in a war with Turkey preferred to relinquish its claim over the management of the games and also its insistence to declare Athens as the permanent venue. Secondly, the victory of Spiridian Loius, a Greek peasant, in the marathon event filled them with such a joy that they forgot about all the jealousies and malice that they were nursing in their bosom on account of sweeping victories by the outsiders and decided to bury the hatchet once and for all. The marathon race, about which more in a subsequent chapter, thus also played a notable role in creating a healthy atmosphere for smooth conduct of future Olympic Games.

As a result, Paris was allotted the 1900 Olympics at the following Olympic Congress which met at Le Havre where a comprehensive plan was chalked out specifying the categories of games to be organised. They were: 1. Ancient Sports of Egypt, India, Greece and Rome; 2. Sports of the Age of Chivalry and 3. Sports of the modern period.

Thus, far things moved smoothly and promised bright prospects of a still better show in Paris. But then the French government intervened decisively and assumed control of the entire organisation. Various committees were formed comprising politicians and other high-ups who had hardly any credentials to offer in the realm of sports organisation. No wonder, therefore, that the resultant show was naturally an assay in mismanagement. The Racing Club de France in the Bois de Boulogue, where the games were held, presented a shabby spectacle where tracks were somehow marked on an irregular surface. To think that the athletes expected a cinder track! Pits for jumping events were conspicuous by their absence. Trajectories of the discus and hammer throws were often obstructed by the trees which could not be felled. In a nutshell, the arrangements would not have done credit even to a collegiate meet. Besides, what should have been the star attraction was held just as a side show to the great Paris Exposition which was going on in the vicinity. The attendance at the games was so poor that even when there was no gate-money the participants easily outnumbered the spectators.

The prospects of the 'tender sappling', which Coubertin and the Greeks had so successfully planted in Athens four years ago, certainly looked bleak. But the redeeming feature of the Paris fiasco was that the inadequacies of the governmental control had been fully exposed once and for all, which helped Coubertine and his Olympic Committee tighten up their hold once again.

The next Olympics moved onto St. Louis in the United States in 1904 but insofar as public reception is concerned the St. Louis Olympics enjoyed no better fate. Once again, the games served just as a side-attraction to the world fair, the Lousisiana Purchase Exposition being held at St. Louis, Missouri. The attendance at the games was far below expectations. And then the greatest drawback was the distance of the venue from the rest of the world, which in that pre-jet age were several weeks away. Consequently, huge financial commitments involved severely restricted the number of European spectators as well as athletes. England which finished second in the Paris Olympics did not send a single athlete. Nor did France and Sweden. It, therefore, turned out to be more or less a local affair for the host country in sharp contrast to an international meet which it was supposed to be. No wonder, the USA had a hey day and came on top in 21 out of the 22 track and field events.

All this did not augur well for the ambitious venture in its infancy. The happenings at the Paris and the St. Louis Olympics dwarfed the stature of the game in no small measure and belied the hopes promised by the splendid success of the Athens games.

Coubertin, quite naturally, was sorely dejected and disappointed as his sincere efforts for a successful international games project seemed to be coming to nought. But exhilarating memories of Athens were a shining streak in the dark. He found himself on the horns of a dilemma between the Greek insistence for a permanent venue and his own stubborn conviction that the games be held in all corners of the world in rotation. The former would make a mockery of the principles he cherished and the latter belittled the Olympic image as the experience of Paris and St. Louis had proved. However, determined as he was, Coubertin overcame his predicament by evolving a via media which was well received by the Greeks as also the rest of the world. Hoping that a return to Athens might give permanency and the much needed impetus to the games, he proposed holding of a mid-Olympic games, the Panhellenic games, to be held every four years in Athens beginning from 1906.

The 1906 Games in Athens recalled the grandeur of the first Olympics of 1896 and were a thumping success. The familiar Greek enthusiasm and the jam-packed crowds in the historic stadium did a lot to restore the vanishing glory and it appeared that the mid-Olympic Games had also come to stay. But the internal political unrest in Greece coupled with the growing demand for facilities at international athletic meets involving huge financial outlay forced the Greeks to abandon the idea and the meet scheduled for 1910 was cancelled. Originally, the Panhellenic Games were supposed to enjoy official status alongwith the regular Olympic games but since they ceased to be held after the first they are no more considered as such. Nevertheless, they always get a listing alongwith the Olympic story.

Although the Paris and the St. Louis Olympics had considerably tarnished the Olympic image, the big cities of the world vied for the honour of hosting them. Originally, the 1908 games were allotted to Rome but owing to unsatisfactory preparations and lack of enthusiasm on the part of Italy the venue had to be shifted to London.

The Fourth Olympics in London truly provided a rich fare and in terms of excellence clearly surpassed the previous three. However, amidst all the grandeur and splendour of the games and excellent arrangements, some ugly incidents resulting from petty jealousies once again marred and almost ruined what must otherwise have been remembered as an ideal Olympics. The London Olympics also failed to impart the solidity which had been eluding the Olympic movement.

It was left to Stockholm to put an end to all misgivings about the future of the Olympic Games. The Swedes by their most methodical and meticulous organisation and efficient conduct of the Games in 1912 not only ensured the Olympic revival but also earned for themselves the distinction of having accomplished what others had failed to achieve. It seemed that the days of teething trouble were over and the Olympic Games had definitely come to stay for good but nobody could have imagined that the First World War (1914) would shake its stability.

8

The Marathon Story

Strange as it may sound yet, prima facie, the marathon race had much to do in rescueing the Olympic Games from a premature death and ridding it of much of its teething troubles. In 1896, the inaugural year, despite the overwhelming enthusiasm evinced by the Greeks and zeroing in of all their resources to revive the Olympic glory, the Greeks seemed to be developing a sort of frenzied antipathy and antagonism towards the Games because of the sweeping victories scored by non-Greeks in almost all the events. The Greek spectators who jam-packed the stadium throughout the run of the games were subjected to the agony of unmitigated humiliation to see their own graceful athletes being repeatedly outclassed by the overseas challenges from America.

But then came the great marathon race on the fifth day of that inaugural year of modern Olympics.

The marathon race had never found a place in the ancient Olympic Games. The longest foot-race known was the Dolichos of 24 stades, i.e. slightly less than three miles.

The idea of holding a long distance race (equivalent to the surface distance from Marathon to Athens) was first mooted at the international Congress in 1894 by one of the French delegates, Michel Breal, who also donated a trophy to commemorate the legendary feat of Pheidippides.

The Pheidippides story dates back to the last decade of the fifth century BC when Darius of Persia sent Hippias to attack Greece (Hellas). Hippias captured Eretria and thereafter landed at Marathon. The Persian Wings, however wilted against the concerted and impetuous attack of the Lacedenians whereupon the main body of the Persians fled to their ships in retreat.

Jubiliant over the victory the Athenian general sent his Olympic champion Pheidippides to convey the good news and relieve the tension of anxious Athens. Badly battered and exhausted as he was by the rubbings in the battle against the Persians, Pheidippides set about the arduous mission — the most glorious race of his life but alas his last. Plodding over the rough, high and low and totally oblivious of his own physical condition, Pheidippides carried out the mission but in the process had spent the last in him. Hardly had he reached the market place in Athens than he dropped dead but not before he had delivered the good news with his last breath. Rejoice we conquer.

On Sunday, 10th April 1896, nearly 2,400 years after Pheidippides historic run, another Greek in the person of Spiridon Louis was covering almost the same route to bring glory to his nation – the glory which indirectly went a long way in establishing the revival of the Olympic Games on a sound footing.

Spiridon Louis, a handsome youth of about 25 years, hailing from the hills of Maroussi; slender, short statured and sporting an impressive moustache, was never a runner of any repute. He was conscripted into the Greek infantry and while serving there was spotted by Colonel M. Papadia- matopoulos (whose name has been especially mentioned here simply for its peculiarity and nothing else) of the regiment for exhibiting extraordinary energy during long route marches. When the first Olympics were on hand the Colonel persuaded Louis to compete in the marathon race for the honour of his country.

It is said that Spiridon Louis spent two nights meditating and praying in front of holy pictures and fasted the day before the race. The fast weakened him physically but purified him spiritually.

The following day at 2 p.m. he was among the 25 starters who took off from the bridge on the outskirts of Marathon, almost the same place where the Persians were made to flee in 490 BC. Among the runners were at least three well known long distance runners, E.H. Flack of Australia, A. Blake of the USA and the Frenchman A. Lermusianus who had finished first, second and third respectively in the 1,500 meters race of the same Olympics. All of them set up a quick pace and forged much ahead of the rest of the field. But all the three got exhausted and gave up one by one – Blake was the first to retire at 15 miles; the Frenchman, who had taken such a big lead that people on the way garlanded and congratulated him taking him for sure winner, collapsed at 20 miles and was transported the rest of the distance in an ambulance. This left only Flack in the lead who seemed to be heading for his third crown (he had already won the 800 metres and 1500 metres). But Spiridon Louis, who was close on his heels with elegant strides, soon overtook him and Flack, too, gave up four miles from the finish, completely exhausted.

Meanwhile, there was intense excitement inside the Panathenaic Stadium where the progress of the race was being relayed through mounted couriers. And when the Colonel who had prevailed upon Spiridon Louis to compete in the race arrived to inform the Royalty and the assembly that Louis was in the lead, the atmosphere was at once electrified — charged with enthusiasm and excitement. Pandemonium broke out and an uproar rose to frenzied heights as soon as the Commissioner of Police, galloped in to announce that Louis had entered the stadium. Crown Prince Constantine and the tall Prince George left the Royal Box in a state of high excitement flanking the plodding Greek, covered the last 200 metres to the finish. Indeed, the entire Greece went wild with joy and in their ecstasy forgot all about the gall and rancour that was gnawing their hearts because of predominance of the foreigners in all the events. And why not, when in the most prestigious race at least, the Greeks had almost completely swept the board and redeemed their honour. Except for the third place which went to G. Killner of Hungary all the first six places were bagged by the Greeks.

The marathon race has since been a glamour attraction at all the subsequent Olympics. Because of the historical aura and the great distance involved the race is run across natural surroundings with only a fraction of the coarse falling inside the main stadium. In Athens it was altogether a different matter with the course of the race being almost exactly the same as covered by Pheidippides in 490 BC. At other places the route is so laid that the distance may approximate to that between Marathon and Athens. The distance has, therefore, been varying marginally from Olympics to Olympics until 1924; thereafter it was standardised and fixed at 26 miles, 385 yards i.e. 42,195 metres.

The distances for which the marathon races were run at different Olympics from 1896 were as under:

1896	Athens	24 miles and 1500 yards or 40,000 metres
1900	Paris	25 miles or 40,260 metres
1904	St. Louis	24 miles and 1500 yards or 40,000 metres
1908	London	26 miles and 385 yards or 42,195 metres
1912	Stockholm	24 miles and 1725 yards or 40,200 metres
1920	Antwerp	26 miles and 990 yards or 42,750 metres
1924	Paris	26 miles and 385 yards or 42,195 metres (standardised since then)

In the marathon race particularly, it is not possible to apply any yardstick to compare performances and timings of the winners at different Olympics. This is so because even after the standardisation of the distance for the race, the terrain, topography and the climate which have a considerable bearing upon the timing, cannot conceivably always be the same at different venues.

In marathon races there has always been an stray incident here and an interesting story there to make a particular Olympics memorable.

To start with, the 1904 Olympic Games in St. Louis offers a case in point. A practical joke, or better still to call it a curious hoax, was perpetrated by Fred Lorz of the USA who was amongst the 31 starters. The race started from the stadium, and after a twelve mile probing course in the country, was to finish again in the stadium. From the start till the runners were in view of the spectators thronging the stadium, Fred was clearly ahead of the rest. The rest of the story relates to 'outdoors'. After toiling for about nine miles in the grueling heat he developed severe cramps and had to retire. He was picked up in one of the accompanying auto-trucks meant for such eventualities. The vehicle being one of those antique pieces, incidentally, also broke down after some distance but not before Fred had a good rest and once again fit enough to run. His clothes were in the stadium and he feared if he waited there stationary in the open, the cramps might well recur. So, to avoid catching cold and stiffening of muscles, he sprinted the remaining five miles to the stadium.

To be fair to Fred, there didn't seem to be any intention of deceipt or deception on his part as it was no secret that he had retired from the race and while on the auto he had been waiving to all the passersby. On his entry into the stadium, however, Fred, as fresh as paint and taking long, elegant strides was greeted with such a thunderous applause and roaring ovation that he couldn't simply resist the temptation and completed the run round the stadium exactly as the real winner would have done. Every one present and witnessing the affair mistook him to be the winner and he didn't do anything to disabuse them. He was even photographed with Miss Alice Roosevelt, daughter of the then American President and was about to receive the prize from her when somebody shouted that he was an imposter and that the genuine runners were way behind.

Poor Fred was debarred for life for trying to be funny.

Then there was the amusing dwarf in the person of Felix Carvajal from Cuba whose carefree gay exuberance and free and innocent mixing won him the admiration and sympathy of everybody he came in contact with. It is said that the diminutive Cuban reported at the starting line in the marathon race in St. Louis in heavy walking shoes, fullsleeved shirt and full pants whereupon hefty Marin Sheridon could not help but play the role of his handler and cut to size the dangling sleeves and trousers to make Fred look anything but a burdened morning walker. It would be natural for anybody to wonder how Felix Carvajal could manage to reach St. Louis, not to say the starting line of an Olympic event. That in itself is a fascinating story.

Felix Carvajal, postman in Havana with no athletic background, became obsessed with the notion that he would be a winner of the Olympic marathon race in St. Louis. Finances for the trip, however, posed a big problem. But he had his own extraordinary way of solving it. He resigned his post of the mail carrier, made public his intended trip to St. Louis and started running for long spells in a public square to attract attention. He besought the interested spectators to contribute liberally and by repeated performances collected sufficient money for a start. Enroute, he indulged in the imprudent act of trying his luck in a game of dice in a club in New Orleans and lost to the last penny. Once again a pauper, he struggled his way on foot, subsisting on the mercy of others, nevertheless, he did reach the venue and was on the starting line.

Quite often in the course of the marathon race Felix led all the rest, chatted, gossiped, cracked jokes with the crowd on the way and ate and drank whatever they offered. In this hilarious, happy-go-lucky attitude he devoured some fresh apples also which caused him cramps and he lost all the lead and was doomed. Nonetheless, it rebounds to the credit of that pygmy amusing freak to have finished fourth in the galaxy of T.J. Hicks, A. J. Corey and A. I. Newton all of the United States.

The field in this historic race in St. Louis also included Lentauw of South Africa who finished ninth despite having being forced to take a detour and run a mile extra in consequence, as he was scared by a big, burly hostile dog during the run. It is anybody's guess what Lentauw might have achieved had he not been chased off the course by canine enemy.

In the London Olympics of 1908, which was marred with frictions and controversies, protests and counter-protests, the finish of the marathon race provided the biggest of them all and hottest. Dorando Pietri of Italy staggered into the stadium ahead of all the rest and was welcomed with a thunderous applause from the stands. Pietri, badly exhausted as he was, got flustered and turned in the wrong direction. The crowd yelled once again; this time in sympathy and in disapproval of his wrong turning, apprehending that by taking a wrong turn his brave efforts might come to nought. Here it may be pointed out that all races on track are run anti-clockwise and, therefore, by force of habit, Pietri on entering the stadium had turned right which was otherwise correct. But for this particular race a deviation from the normal practice was made as the finishing line was set before the reviewing stand, which meant that the runners would have to make an unusual left turn as they entered the stadium. Utterly shocked, bewildered and completely exhausted Pietri collapsed on the track. There was a general hue and cry; some sympathetic urgings to lend the fallen athlete a helping hand and some warnings not to touch him lest he should be disqualified. In the resulting confusion the British Officials first hovered around him and then hesitatingly helped him on his feet and guided him towards the right direction. Pietri tottered along a short distance and collapsed again. Officials once again lent a helping hand and with three more such assistance Pietri managed to touch the finishing line. The crowd gave him a big ovation for his gallant effort and while the applause for Pietri rent the air, Johny Hayes of the USA, a slim young chap with plenty of steam still on was trundling unaided and crossed over the finishing line almost unnoticed.

There should have been no doubt that Dorando Pietri stood disqualified and Johny Hayes was the winner. But the officials took hours to decide that Johny Hayes was the winner. In the meanwhile, however, the Italian flag had already been unfurled at the top of the pole (followed by the American) heralding the Italian as the winner of that prestigious race.

Ultimately, however, Johny Hayes, got the gold medal. Pietri, too, was amply rewarded, unofficially though, when the very next day Queen Alexandra presented him with a gold cup in appreciation of his outstanding courage.

So, Michel Breal, by mooting the idea of introducing the marathon race and donating a trophy for the purpose not only set an institution which provided stability to the Olympic Games, though indirectly, but also enriched the sports world with an event which has always been, and will ever be, eventful and replete with interesting stories, thrills, turns and twists.

Wonder why there couldn't be another 'Breal' to have been inspired by the feat of Argeus, a long distance runner of the ancient Olympic Games. Argeus, on winning the 'Dolichos' race of 24 lengths of the stade, ran all the way from Olympia to Argos, his hometown, a distance of 34 miles, to tell his girl friend that he had won an Olympic championship.

9

Some Basic Facts

Before proceeding further with our story and recount the highlights and landmarks of the first few modern Olympic Games which laid the foundation of these games on a firm footing, it will not be out of place to acquaint the readers with some important facts about the conduct of these games vis-à-vis its counter part in ancient games which might be interesting and informative at the same time. What follows therefore, is an enumeration of some basic facts and figures concerning some of the many events in the modern Olympic Games.

DISCUS – It weights 2 kilogrammes or 4 lbs. 6.4 oz. It is a circular wooden disc whose edge is reinforced with smooth metal ring around it and brass plates set inside. For women, the weight of discuss is 2.2 lbs (1 kg.).

SHOT-PUT – The spherical weight heaved in the shot-put item is made of solid iron, or brass or a shell made of any metal not softer than brass, filled with lead. It weights 16 lbs. (7.257 kgs). For ladies, the weight is 8.8 lbs. (4 kgs.).

HAMMER – The hammer in the hammer throw event is not exactly a hammer nor any thing like that. Even then it is named as such though in effect it consists of a spherical iron or spherical ball, approximately half the size of a football, connected with a swivel chain and ending in a loop so as to provide for a firm grip.

The whole length of this 'hammer' from the loop for the grip to the weight must not be more than 4 feet. The total weight is 16 lbs. (7.257 kgs.) in all.

JEVELIN – The spear meant to be hurled in ancient times, both by infantry and cavalry, is called javelin. It is a long, circular wooden spear not less than 8 ft. 6 inches (2.60 metres) in length and made out of the logs of birch tapering to a sharp iron or steel point. For a proper grip and easy handling of the long javelin, a whipcord, without any fastener or thongs, is wrapped at the centre of gravity, which is located at about 3 ft. to 3½ ft. from the foremost point. The weight of the javelin used in men's event is not less than 1 lb. 12/ ¼ oz. (800 grammes).

POLE VAULT – For the poles to be used in the pole vault event there are no prescribed specifications as regards its length, thickness or the material it should be made of. Consequently, poles made of any kind of suitable wood, bamboo or aluminium, with metal spike affixed at one end, and length of their own choice, are generally used by pole vaulters. With the advanced techniques of late, however, pole vaulters in high competitions are using poles made of plexiglass or fiberglass which gives them more whip off the ground in their take-off.

RACES – For races, cinder tracks are now used in place of the grass tracks which were lately in vogue. All short races upto 120 yards must be run on flat or straight course, the width of which should not be less than 4 feet. Longer races are run on oval shaped tracks, the distances on which are calculated from a point one foot outside of the inner edge which demarcates the lanes.

In relay races, the baton which exchanges hands and is relayed through runners, is a smooth, circular piece 12 inches in length, made of wood or metal and hollow inside so that its weight approximates 1/ ¾ oz.

HURDLE RACE – There are ten obstacles to be crossed over in hurdle races. In the 110 metres or 120 yards hurdles race the hurdles are placed at intervals of 10 yards (9.14 meters) with the first hurdle at a distance of 15 yards (13.72 metres) from the starting point. The last hurdle is placed at a distance of 15 yards 1 foot (14.02 metres) from the finish. The effective height of each hurdle is 3 feet, 6 inches (1.06 metres). The hurdles are so designed as to weigh 22 lbs. 3/ ½ oz. each and it would take at least a force equivalent to 8 lbs. to topple it.

In the 80 metres hurdle for women the hurdles are 2 ½ feet (72.6 cms) high and are placed 8 metres apart with the first hurdle 12 metres from the starting line and the last also 12 metres from the finish; eight hurdles in all.

The hurdles used in 400 metres or 440 yards race are six inches shorter in height and are placed 38/ ¼ yards (35 metres apart from one another with the first one 49/ ¼ yards (45 metres) from the starting line and the last one 43/ ¼ yards (40 metres) from the finish.

STEEPLE CHASE – In the steeple chase item the hurdles are 3 feet high. There are five such hurdles to be negotiated in each lap out of which at least one should have a water pit.

It is the finishing line marked on the ground across the width of the tracks that is the crucial line for determining the winners in track races and not the tape. The tape which is stretched 4 feet just above the finishing line is, therefore, only for the assistance of the judges which also incidentally serves as a indicator to the runners from a distance the extent upto which they have to run.

WRESTLING AND WEIGHT LIFTING – In the wrestling and weight-lifting events which are essentially measures of individual strength, the competitions are held, and competitors are classified, in different weight groups so that disparities are eliminated and as far as possible individuals with approximately equal weights only are pitched against one another. The different groups in which competitions are held have been standardised. They are (the weights given in brackets are the maximum for each group).

Bantam weight (123 ½ lbs.),

Feather weight (132 ½ lbs.),

Middle weight (165 ¾ lbs.),

Light heavy weight (181 7/8 lbs.)

Middle heavy weight (198 3/8 lbs.), and Heavy weight (unlimited).

In the wrestling event, competitions are held in the two recognised styles of wrestling: (1) The Greco-Roman style bequeathed by the ancient Olympics in which only holds above the waist are allowed, and (2) the catch-as-catch-can, of American orign in which, as the name suggests no holds are barred.

HORSE RIDING – In the equestrian events, competitions are held in three disciplines, viz., dressage, the three-day riding test, and show jumping. In all these events, individual as well as team championships are held so that there are three individual prizes in each competition and three prizes for teams. Accordingly, three riders and three horses may compete from each participating country in each of the three events separately.

For the dressage competition, each rider is required to perform a set of predetermined exercises in 13 minutes.

The three day test event, as the name suggests is spread over three days of gruelling tests which are to be performed by the same rider on the same horse. On the first day, a dressage test is held in which each competitor has to perform a series of pre-set exercises in 12 minutes. On the second day, the riders have to cover a total of approximately 20 miles on road, tracks steeplechase course, cross-country with many obstacles, and flat surfaces with very little time allowed in between. On the third day, the same set of riders who underwent such nerve breaking contests the previous days are required to jump over a course of 12 obstacles at a speed of 440 yards per minute.

The third competition in the equestrian events consists mainly of show jumps over difficult hurdles and obstacles numbering nearly 20. This event is popularly known as Prix des Nations.

FENCING – In the fencing events competitions in three types of weapons are held – 1. Foil, 2. Epee, and 3. Sabre. In all these, the basic object is the same, i.e., a competitor tries to touch his opponent with the specified part of the weapon and at the same time avoid himself to be so touched by the opponent. In the foil, touches with the weapon are allowed on the opponents body only from the collar to the hiphone line. In epee, a touch can be made on any part of opponents body, from top to toe. In Saber, touches are allowed only above the waist of the opponent.

In all the fencing events, the contestants put on proper protective clothing with masks, gloves, etc.

MODERN PENTATHLON – The modern pentathon comprises competitions in five sports, viz., running, riding, shooting, fencing and swimming. It is a very gruelling contest in which competitive efficiency in all these sports is a must. A modern pentathlon competitor is required to run 4,000 metres cross-country, ride on untrained horse allotted by lot at the commencement of the event, over 5,000 metres steeple chase course made up of 30 jumps, to compete in rapid fire pistol shooting at running silhouette targets from 25 metres with any type of .22 caliber pistol, to fence with a sword and to swim 300 metres free style. Save for the fencing item, in the remaining four items the contest is not between contestants, but against time. The timings so returned arc converted into points from a standard table.

INTERNATIONAL OLYMPIC COMMITTEE – The International Olympic Committee (IOC) is the supreme body which governs the Olympic Games. It was founded on June 13, 1894 at the International Congress of Paris which authorised and made the IOC responsible for:

1. The regular celebrations of the Games.
2. Making these Games increasingly perfect, more and more worthy of their glorious past and in keeping with the high ideals that inspired those who revived them.
3. The encouragement or organisations of all events and, in general, the taking of all steps likely to lead modern athletics along the right lines.

The IOC which consists of a number of co-opted members, is headed by a president who is elected by majority for a period of eight years.

The president of the IOC is assisted by three vice-presidents who are elected for four-year terms. They alongwith five other elected members form the executive committee which is the seat of all decisions.

The IOC is a 'self-recruiting body' and therefore recruits its own members – not more than one from each country having a National Olympic Committee, or in special cases two.

A member is elected on the recommendations of the executive board, which proposes his name for approval of the general meeting. On being elected, the member of the IOC is required to take the following oath:

> 'Recognising the responsibilities that go with the great honour of being elected a member of the IOC and representing it in my country, I undertake to promote the Olympic Movement to the best of my ability, to respect and safeguard the fundamental principles of the Olympic Charter as conceived by Baron Pierre de Cobertin, and to remain free of any political or commercial pressures as well as of any considerations of race or religion.'

The most important and noteworthy characteristic of an IOC member is that he is not a delegate of his country to the IOC; instead he represents the IOC in his own country.

This aspect is in fact responsible for the IOC being such an independent, impartial and permanent organisation, not easily influenced by any political pressures or racial prejudices. A general meeting of the IOC known as a session is held once a year, (twice in years when the Games are held); at this session members elect the board of directors called the executive board.

The general meeting is governed by an agenda which includes, *inter alia*, the following main points :

(i) Election of the president, vice president and members of the executive board, the co-opting of new members.

(ii) Selection of town (every four years) which will organise the next Olympic Games;

(iii) Modifications, if necessary to the Olympic rules and regulations;

(iv) The recognition of new National Olympic Committees;

(v) Examination of the requests of the International Federations; and

(vi) General review of the effects of international politics on sports.

Each country which is a member of the IOC has a National Olympic Committee which serves as a sort of a national arm of the IOC. Each National Committee is composed of the representatives of different national sports federations which in turn are affiliated with international federations, and the IOC delegate from that country, if there is one. Only these national Olympic Committees can judge the eligibility of athletes for participation in the Olympic Games.

The IOC grants the organisation of the Games to the National Olympic Committee of the country of the Games, host city. It is significant that the Games are allotted to cities and not the countries in which they are situated.

The IOC chooses and finalises the venue of future Olympic Games six years in advance.

The Olympic Movement, having accomplished international character and representation, has developed into a big complex requiring specialised attention on widely different and diversified aspects. It has to rely on specialists for the completion of its programmes and in the achievement of its aims. In order, therefore, to equip itself with the experience and thus simplify its task, the IOC calls on special commissions to deal with specific problems. Some of the commissions are as under:-

Finance commission; press and public relations commission; legislation commission; eligibility commission; commission for the international Olympic Academy; cultural commission; commission for the protection of the Olympic emblems; medical commission; tripartite commission for the preparation of the Olympic Congress; and joint commission for the Olympic programme.

10

Awards and Ceremonies

To popularise the Olympic Movement, as also to give incentive and acknowledge the services rendered by individuals or organisations, the IOC offers a number of awards in token of its appreciation. A brief description of the major trophies is given below:

The Olympic Cup, founded by Baron de Coubertin in 1906, is awarded to an institution or association of a general and disinterested character that has rendered eminent services to the cause of sport or that has successfully contributed to the spreading of the Olympic ideal. The cup is kept at the IOC headquarters; the recipient of the award is given a bronze plaque and a diploma.

The Olympic Diploma of Merit, created at the Brussels Congress in 1905, is awarded to an individual satisfying the same conditions as those indicated above for the Olympic Cup; the only difference between the two awards is that whereas the Olympic Cup is for institutions or associations the Diploma of Merit is for individuals.

The Fearnley Cup, founded in 1950 by Sir Thomas Fearnley, is given to an amateur sports club, or a local amateur sports association, for meritorious achievement in the service of the Olympic Movement. The cup is kept at the IOC headquarters; the recipient of the award is given a miniature and diploma.

The Mohammad Tahir Trophy, founded in 1950 by H.E. Mohammad Tahir, is awarded to an amateur athlete who may or may not have competed in the Olympic Games but whose general merit or career merits the award of a special distinction. The trophy is kept at the IOC headquarters; the recipient of the award is given a plaque and a diploma.

The Count Bonacossa Trophy, created by the Italian National Olympic Committee and the family of the late Alberto Bonacossa, is awarded to a National Olympic Committee that has done outstanding work in furthering the Olympic Movement. The trophy is kept at the IOC headquarters; the recipient of the award receives a miniature and a diploma.

The Tokyo Trophy, offered in 1964 by the city of Tokyo, is awarded to an athlete (or a group of athletes) whose behaviour during the Olympic Games is exemplary and may be called as an example of outstanding sportsmanship irrespective of actual results. The trophy is kept at the IOC headquarters; the recipient of the award receives a miniature and a diploma.

The headquarters of the IOC is in Lausanne, Switzerland. The Chateau de Vidy, which houses the headquarters, is situated just off the road by the Lake of Geneva between Lausanne and St. Sulpice. The Chateau was graciously placed at the disposal of the IOC by the town of Lausanne in 1968.

The Emblems: The IOC emblem is composed of five interlaced rings, each of a different colour; blue, yellow, black, green and red, so placed that the blue ring is nearest to the flag pole. The scheme of the five coloured rings is fixed so that the yellow ring slightly lowered connects the blue and black. Similarly, the green ring which follows the black is also slightly lowered and connects black and red. Coubertin, who designed this emblem in 1913, explained its symbolism in the following words:

'These five rings, blue, yellow, black, green and red, represent the five parts of the world which from now on belong to the Olympic Movement and which are ready to accept the fruitful

rivalry it entails. In addition, the combination of the six colours (counting the white background) represents every nation without exception. The blue and yellow of Sweden, the blue and white of Greece, the French, English, American, German, Belgium, Italian and Hungarian tricolours, the yellow and red of Spain touching the New Brazilian and Australian, with ancient Japan and young China. A truly 'international emblem.'

The original flag whose dimensions are three metres long and two metres wide was made in the 'Bon Marche' store, adjoining the birth place of Coubertin. The flag has a white background with no border. In the centre of the flag is the Olympic emblem – the five interlaced rings spread over two metres in length and 60 centimeters in width.

The Olympic flag made its first official appearance in 1914 when it was presented by Baron de Coubertin at the Olympic Congress at Paris. It was first hoisted at an Olympic Stadium during the Antwerp Games in 1920. Just below the rings is written the Olympic motto: 'Citius, Altius. Fortius' meaning 'Faster, Higher, Stronger'. The motto was coined way back in 1890 by Father Didon, a pedagogue by profession and a close friend of Coubertin by inclination. An enthusiastic promoter of sports in schools in the late nineteenth century, Father Didon appreciated the importance of sports in the moulding of his pupils. But he could have never imagined then that the motto, which he dedicated to the sporting club founded by him, would achieve the unique distinction of becoming part and parcel of the Olympic Movement. The flag, the rings, and the motto are the exclusive property of the IOC and cannot be used without its consent.

Opening ceremony: The opening ceremony of the games follows a traditional pattern which is both impressive and stirring. Since the very beginning of the modern Games, it starts with the reception of a sovereign or a Head of State in the stadium by the President of the IOC. The officials of the organising committee are then introduced to the sovereign or the head of state that is then conducted to the Tribune of Honour. The massed bands and choirs then start rendering the national anthem of the country to which the organising city belongs. This is followed by the colourful and captivating procession of athletes (country-wise) in alphabetical order for the traditional march-past. Since 1920, Greece, as the founder of the Games, has led the march with the organising country forming the rear. The standard bearers while passing in front of the Tribune of Honour dip their flags and the contingent following turn their 'eyes right' in salute. The parade over, and after the athletes and officials have settled in the middle of the stadium, the president of the IOC, with a brief speech of welcome, requests the Chief of State to declare the games open who makes the customary 16-words proclamation: 'I declare open the Olympic Games of … (name of city), celebrating the (number of Olympiad) Olympiad of the modern era.'

A fanfare of trumpets is sounded and to the strains of the Olympic anthem, composed in 1896 by the Greek Spirou Samara, with words by Costis Palamas, the Olympic flag is slowly raised on the central mast. The official flag (in embroidered satin, donated in 1920 by the Belgian Olympic Committee) is handed over by a representative of the city in which the preceding games were held, to the President of the IOC who passes it on to the mayor of the organising city. This flag is kept in the principal municipal building until the next Games.

Roaring of guns and the release of thousands of pigeons herald the commencement of the games. Traditionally the release of pigeons is symbolic of peace and international amity.

The Olympic Flame: Intended to burn throughout the Games, the flame, lit in the sun at Olympia and relayed by thousands of runners now enters the stadium. The prestige and honour attached to the carrying of the Olympic torch is such that athletes vie for this honour.

It was in Amsterdam in 1928 that a flame first burnt throughout the run of the Olympic Games. However, it was not until 1936 that at the suggestion and initiative of Carl Diem of Germany, the traditional ceremony in vogue now was organised at Olympia.

The choice of the last bearer of the torch, i.e., the athlete who brings the torch inside the stadium and lits the bowl specially meant for the purpose, often has a symbolic character. The athlete, after entering into the stadium takes a round of the stadium with the torch held aloft in hand and then climbs the flights of steps leading to the highest point where the bowl is kept. Plunging the torch into the bowl, the athlete brings to life the flames which leap and flutter until the Games last.

The Oaths: After the flame has been lit and the stage set for the commencement of the Games, an athlete of the host country advances to the rostrum accompanied by the flag-bearer of his country. He raises his right hand and takes the oath on behalf of all the participants: 'In the name of all competitors, I promise that we will take part in these Olympic Games, respecting and abiding by the rules which govern them, in the true spirit of sportsmanship, for the glory of sport and the honour of our teams'. The oath was taken for the first time at the VII Olympic Games at Antwerp in 1920.

A similar ceremony is held for the officials and judges who swear to: 'Officiate with complete impartiality, respecting and abiding by the rules which govern them, in the true spirit of sportsmanship.'

The national anthem of the host country is then played marking the end of the openıng ceremony and the entire assembly of athletes, officials and delegates who had stationed themselves in the middle of the stadium now leave to clear the ground for the start of the Games.

The Awards: With the narration so far of the procedure followed in the current Olympic Games, a close similarity must have been noticed with the practices which were in vogue in the ancient Olympic Games: the continuous burning of the fire during the run of the games, the oath taking ceremonies by the participants and the judges for fair play and impartiality. In the matter of prizes, however, the purely symbolic olive leaves of old are nowadays replaced by medals. These are awarded immediately after the event wherever possible and in accordance with a ceremony laid down in the rules of the Olympic Games.

The first three competitors in each event take their places on a stand facing the Tribune of Honour with the winner slightly higher, the second on his right and the third on his left. The President of the IOC places the medals – gold for the first, silver for the second and bronze for the third. The flags are then hoisted, that of the winner on the central flag pole and those of the second and third on adjoining flag poles, and national anthem of the winners is played.

The medals awarded to the first three victors have on the reverse side a pattern designed by the Italian artist, Giuseppe Cassisti in 1928. The choice of design for the obverse rests with the organising committee subject, of course, to the approval of the IOC. The first six competitors in each event are given diplomas. Besides the prizes to the winners, a commemorative medal is awarded to all the participants and officials as a token and momento. Finally, the names of the winners are engraved on the walls of the main stadium soon after the Games are over.

The Closing Ceremony: The closing ceremony, the crowning moment of the Games, assumes a special significance; the close linking of brotherhood and hope.

The ceremony is held in the main stadium. The flag-bearers take their place on grass in the centre of the stadium. The athletes, a maximum of six from each delegation, without distinction of nationality, assemble for the last time onto the track where they had confronted each other.

To the strains of the Greek national anthem, the Greek flag is then hoisted to the right of the central flagpole on which hangs the Olympic flag while the flag of the country which has been chosen to organise the next Games is hoisted to the left flagpole, and the national anthems of these two countries are played successively. The President of the IOC then thanks the Head of State, the people and the municipal authorities and the organising committee. He proclaims the closure of the Games of the current Olympiad and invites the youth of all countries to assemble four years hence in the city chosen to celebrate the next Games. A fanfare is then sounded and the sacred Olympic fire is extinguished. The Olympic flag is lowered from the flagpole to the strains of the Olympic anthem and is carried horizontally from the arena. A salute of five guns is fired and the choir sings a song of farewell.

11

ATHENS 1896
First Modern Olympics

To say that the first modern Olympic Games held in Athens in 1896 pieced up the thread snapped fifteen centuries earlier will be a truth, meaningful, appropriate and to the point.

The institution of the ancient Olympic Games was revived in the modern set-up with almost the same zeal and reverence that it enjoyed in the days bygone. Fortunately, the evils and corrupt practices which had raised their ugly heads during the last phase of the ancient Olympic Games and which ultimately rang the death knell of that time honoured festival, did not manifest themselves in the inaugural Olympiad of the modern era.

The sky overcast with clouds on that historic day, April 6, 1896, which incidentally was Easter Monday and also the 75th anniversary of Greece's independence from Turkish rule. Since morning, there was bustling activity on all the roads, leading to the ancient stadium of Herodia, now fully renovated, with a seething mass of humanity converging on the venue of the Games being held to mark the revival of that masterpiece of Greek civilisation.

Well before the formal opening, some 50,000 spectators had jam-packed the stadium and almost equal number had occupied vantage positions on the slopes of the surrounding hills, content with whatever distant glimpse of the grand spectacle they could steal by looking down over the walls of the stadium.

King George I of Greece, with Queen Olga and other members of royality all-attention in the royal box, and members of the Diplomatic Corps all around him, formally proclaimed the opening of the first International Olympic Games in Athens. The Games were finally on; and undoubtedly the happiest man on earth at that moment was the tiny Baron de Coubertin whose cherished dreams had come true and untiring life-long efforts fructified at last.

Of the 34 nations, which had endorsed Coubertin's proposal in 1894 for the revival of the Games, only 13 participated. The participating countries were Australia, Bulgaria, Chile, Denmark, Germany, Greece, France, United States, Austria, Great Britain, Switzerland, Sweden and Hungary.

Competitions in nine sports were gone through in the inaugural Olympiad. They were: track and field, fencing, weight lifting, tennis, cycling, wrestling, shooting, swimming and gymnastics. Initially, competitions in rowing were also scheduled to be held but were subsequently cancelled because of bad weather.

James Brendan Connolly of the USA, who later became famous as a writer of sea tales, achieved the unique distinction of becoming the first winner in the series of the first modern Olympic Games and thus picked up the chain of Olympic winners which was broken after Varastades had won an Olympic title 1511 years ago in 385 AD. It so happened that the first final of any event on the opening day was that of the triple jump, popularly known as hop, step and jump. Connolly covered a meager 13.71 metres, a distance that would not even have qualified him for participation in the Games today. Nevertheless, he won the gold medal and became the first ever winner of the modern Olympic Games. In passing, it would be worthwhile mentioning that in those days a triple jumper was allowed to take two hops and a jump in contrast to present day rules which specify a hop, a step, and a jump.

The only other championship decided on the first day also went to the USA. Curiously enough, Bob Garret, who won the discus throw event, had not even seen a discus until his arrival in Greece. In fact, in those days throwing the discus was not known outside Greece. Even so, three Danes, an Englishman, an American, a German, a Swede and a Frenchman alongwith three Greeks competed in the event. Garret, who had been fascinated by the action pictures of this event, had a model of the disc designed by one of his friends, which he used to hurl in practice sessions in New Jersey. But when he was arrayed in the competition, he discovered to his pleasant surprise that the disc to be hurled was much lighter and easier to handle than the rough imitation he had been practicing with. Consequently, he heaved the discus much farther than the best attempt of Paraskevopolos, the Greek champion and the favourite for winning the event. The Greeks, albeit, were credited with full marks for grace but Garret led the field by eight inches. Garret later won the shot put event also.

On the following days, the contingent from the USA continued to dominate the track and field events. Thomas Burke won both the 100 and 400 metre races and Ellery Clark jumped too high and too long to win both the jumping events. Tom Curtis sailed over the hurdles with neatness and despatch to leave the field behind in the 110 metres hurdle race. The pole vault event was won by W.T. Hoyt when he cleared the bar at the height of 10 feet 9¾ inches, — a poor performance if judged by the present day standard but it won him gold medal all the same.

The monotony of the American's run-away victories in track and field events was broken here and there by stray victories of other national athletes. Australian Edwin Flack, romped home in the 800 and 1,500 metre races. And then there was Spiridon Louis who won the most prestigious race, the marathon, for Greece, described in detail in an earlier chapter. There was so much of rejoicing and jubiliation over the Greeks triumph in the marathon that the pole vault event which was in progress was partially interrupted and, in the process, the first and second spots hit by the Americans with the help of poles of extraordinary length went almost unnoticed and unapplauded. William Hyot of the USA sailed over the bar 3.30 metres high which was a fabulous height for the event in those days.

The cycling events consisted of six items, four of which were won by Frenchmen, — Paul Masson winning the first three short distance ones. The cycling marathon dished out some spectacular moment and a feast of drama. The six competitors started from Athens for marathon where they were required to sign on a parchment before a Special Commissioner and then return to the Velodrome in Athens. The ultimate winner, A. Konstantinidis of Greece, experienced many ordeals before pedaling to victory. Not only did he have the handicap of a lengthy signature but as soon as he commenced his return lap, his cycle broke down. Undeterred, he took the starter's cycle lying handy and started speeding towards Athens. But this bike, too went out of order and threw down the cyclist. Undaunted and determined, Konstantinidis snatched a friend's cycle and pedaled home to victory, a neat 20 minutes ahead of his nearest rival.

The performances put in by athletes in Athens in 1896 were not worthy of an Olympic meet. The reasons were not far to seek. The athletes in those far away days were not so well trained, scientifically and otherwise, as they are today nor were sporting events so systematically organised. The stadium where the Olympic Games were staged was more of a show-piece of antiquity than a sports arena. It was almost an exact replica of an ancient Greek stadium. The oval track had so sharp turns that the cancellation of the 200 metre run was very prudent step otherwise the runners in full blast would not have been able to contain themselves while negotiating the curves and possibly would have collided with disastrous results. Besides, the tracks were sandy and did not provide the firm foothold required for athletic excellence.

Facilities and performing conditions in other events were also far from satisfactory and left plenty to be desired. Swimmers, used to the warm water of swimming pools, had to bear the biting chill of the icy waters of the Bay of Zea where even the starting and finishing lines were not distinctly defined. An American competitor for the 100 metres swimming event gave up immediately on entering into the icy cold water, screaming: 'I am freezing, I am freezing'. Besides, the competitors, as also the officials, had to be constantly on guard against the risk of drowning.

The first of the modern Olympic Games held more than hundred years ago are to be judged in the circumstances obtaining then and not by present day standards. The venue of the Games for 1896 was decided only two years earlier in 1894 and immediately the Greek authorities found themselves confronted with the problems of adequate funds for organising such an international meet. Thanks however, to a wind fall donation of a million drachmas (equivalent to approximately 40,000) from George Averoff, a wealthy Greek philanthropist living in Alexandria coupled with the receipt from commemorative stamps which somehow made possible giving a fresh look to the 2,000 years old Pan-Athenaic Stadium of Heredis. The Greeks, therefore, did not have sufficient time for any sort of advance planning or publicity. Consequently, it was no surprise if one stumbled at instances of sheer farce and casual approaches.

For instance, the 13-member American team, which ultimately romped home with eleven first places could reach Athens after a very tiring, long journey only on the eve of the commencement of the Games, although they thought they would reach the venue at least 10 days in advance. The reason for this confusion was that the Americans were not aware that Greece was still following the Jublian Calendar which differed from the Gregorian by eleven days. And then with the traditional Greek hospitality persuading the American contingent to drink innumerable toasts and other merry-making late into the night and till the crack of dawn, the Americans could not have any rest or respite and had almost to go straight to the stadium for the opening ceremony.

Yet another evidence of a casual approach was the tennis tournament. Anybody could enter and play at the last moment. It was held in the improvised shed on the shores of Illissos. P. Boland of Great Britain who just happened to be there preferred to chance his arms, and lo, and behold, he won!

All the shortcomings notwithstanding, the efforts of reviving the Olympic Games were more than successful. There was overwhelming public enthusiasm with crowds overflowing the stadium on all the days. Despite the mediocre perfomances, Coubertin's ideal which aimed at youths of the world meeting on a friendly field of combat had been duly achieved. A beginning had been made and that was not a small achievement, no matter even if the newspapers did not give it the importance it deserved.

A gold medal and an olive branch were presented by King George to each champion on the tenth and concluding day of the Games in pouring rain. Runners up were awarded a bronze medal and an olive branch. To bid farewell and mark the end of the festivities a valedictory Greek ode, especially composed, was recited by Sir George Stuart Robertson, the Greek scholar and the contestants and the officials were treated to a royal breakfast hosted by the King of Greece.

12

PARIS 1900
Mockery of the Games

If the splendid success of the first Olympic Games at Athens raised hopes of a bright future of the Olympic movement, the exercise in Paris was not only an essay in mismanagement which besmirched its image and lowered its prestige to the lowest level, but also threatened its future.

The games were allotted to Paris in the teeth of stiff opposition from Greece which insisted upon Athens to be its permanent venue. But Coubertin's ideals demanded that the Games should be organised in all the corners of the world by rotation. The response of the French authorities, however, was one of cool indifference, either because they were busy, heart and soul, in the big Paris exposition fair which was going on at the same time (The Paris Exposition of 1900 lasted from May 20 to October 28) or because France still lacked sports awakening so necessary for hosting such an international sporting event.

As a result, the status of the Olympic Games was reduced to no more than a side attraction to the world fair. Still worse, the Games were so casually reported and so loosely talked about that some where in the process the Olympic nomenclature was dropped and it went unnoticed even when the Games were so often referred to as the 'International sports and physical exercise competition'.

Ultimately Coubertin had to intervene and had successfully restored the prefix 'Olympics', but that was only on paper and mattered little when it came to actual organisation and conduct of the Games, as the arrangements made were totally unbecoming of an Olympic meet.

The track and field competitions were held on the grounds of the Racing Club de France in the Bois de Boulogne. To say that the conditions provided for the events were far from satisfactory would be gross understatement. On the green lawns of a small open field known as the Pre Catalan, a team of tired and bored French officials, or so they looked, had simply marked off a course which was to serve as the track for the sprint events. Not to mention the absence of the cinder track, sprint course was not even properly levelled. No pits were provided for the jumping events. It was left to the contestants to help themselves to the extent they could with their own feet and spikes. What was still worse, when the strongmen heaved the discus or hurled the hammer in the throwing events they had the mortification of seeing their best efforts either intercepted by tree tops or landing in the thick of a grove which could not be cleared because the growth there was considered more important than the performance of the athletes in an Olympic event !

Performing conditions apart, the Games in Paris were plagued by a bitter controversy that had started even before they were underway.

Since in continental Europe Sunday was considered as the most appropriate day for sports and recreational pursuits, the French officials had fixed Sunday, July 15 for the opening ceremony. The contingent from the USA however, was more puritan in their outlook and beliefs. They were aghast at the very thought of desecrating the Sabbath and raised vehement protests to the schedule. They even threatened withdrawal unless the programme was modified.

The French officials, even though surprised at the typical orthodoxy of the contestants from across the Atlantic, could have nipped the controversy in bud by advancing the opening ceremony by a day. But that was July 14, a sacred day for the French, being the anniversary of the fall of Bastille when the general public would be watching the military parade. They were thus on the horns of a dilemma and uncertainty prevailed until Wednesday, July 11, when an agreement was reached.

The French, a trifle upset by the adamant attitude and tough stand taken by the US athletes, thought it prudent to yield and agreed to hold the opening ceremony on Saturday with the stipulation that the Sabbath observers would have a chance to compete on Monday against the timings or distances returned on Sunday by athletes who had no such religious convictions.

The compromise helped to bury the hatchet temporarily and the opening of the Games on Saturday had a smooth sailing.

All the same, public enthusiasm was sadly wanting. The stands, wore a deserted look so much so that contestants in the middle outnumbered the spectators. This was understandable in view of what the French officials had foretold about the preoccupation elsewhere of the Parisians on that Bastille Day. But this was an alibi that could hardly hold good even for that particular day as the crowds were conspicuous by their absence throughout the run of the Games. The fact of the matter was that the Games had been given little or no publicity: nor was there any awakening in France in the realm of sports and for this reason these athletic competitions could at best play the second fiddle and were considered to be only a part and parcel of the great Paris Exposition of 1900; in a nutshell, there was nothing of importance beyond a side show which hardly provided any attraction for the natives of France.

The finals of the two races run on the opening day were both won by the Americans. The first was Alvin C Kraenzlein who taped ahead of all in the 110 metres hurdle race rather effortlessly and thus won the first of his four gold medals. In hurdling he is credited with the introduction of the leg-extended style for sailing over the hurdles. Then F. W. Jarvis sprinted the 100 metres in the record time of 10.3 seconds after Arthur Duffy, another fellow American, world record holder and hot favourite for the distance, pulled a tendon midway and was doomed.

Despite the fact that Jarvis and Tewksbury had returned the then world record time of 10.8 seconds in the heats and semi-finals respectively, the 4 ft. 7 inches Arthur Duffy continued to be the favourite for the event as he had beaten both of them in London only a week earlier. In the final, Duffy, quite expectedly, went into the lead early on, but midway to the surprise of all, started wobbling and fell on the ground. Later, he recapitulated his downfall thus: "I do not know why my leg gave way. I felt a peculiar twitching after going twenty yards. I then seemed to lose control of it, and suddenly it gave out, throwing me on my face. But that is one of the fortunes of sport, and I cannot complain". Two years later Duffy set a world record of 9.6 secs. for 100 yards which remained unsurpassed for the next 24 years but could never win the Olympics 100-metres title. Duffy later became a columnist for the 'Boston Post'.

On the conclusion of the first day's programme, the US athletes were in for a shock. Word reached them that the agreement reached earlier regarding observance of Sabbath could not be sustained following pressures and protests from athletes who had no such religious qualms and the programme originally fixed prior to the so called compromise would be adhered to, which in effect meant ten finals on Sunday. Heated debates in the US camp failed to achieve unanimity and there was a split; some finding the lure of competition too tempting to resist.

The US athletic prowess was proved in no uncertain manner when even with a truncated representation, and with a host of their star performers on the sidelines, they bagged as many as eight 'firsts' out of the ten that were won on Sunday. They continued to romp home in the track and field events on the following day, too, and their final tally was 17 'firsts' out of the 23. Of the remaining six, four were won by Great Britain and one each by France and Hungary.

The two athletes who stole the limelight were AC Kraenzlein and RC Ewry both of USA. Kraenzlein won three sprint events – 60 metres flat, 110 and 200 metres hurdles, and the running broad jump and thus achieved the unique distinction of being the first and the only athlete to have won four individual championships in the same year in the history of the track and field events of the Olympic Games.

Ray Ewry's emergence as an athlete par excellence was as remarkable as his fight back to physical perfection from a state of disability which had rendered him invalid even when he was a small boy. His case was almost hopeless, but he was bucked-up not to despair, - and he did not. He stuck religiously to the few exercises suggested to him by his family physician and grew into a tall lanky fellow standing 6 feet 3 inches. His jumping exercises developed him into a star jumper and on a single day, i.e., July 16, 1900 he jumped to fame by winning the three jumping events in a row - the standing high jump, the standing broad jump and the standing hop, step and jump.

Despite such overwhelming dominance of US athletes in track and field items, France still managed to occupy the pride of place by annexing championships in many other disciplines, some of which were unknown in other countries.

The traditionally spectacular marathon race was won by a local baker boy, Michel Teato, who had developed stamina and a pair of agile legs in the performance of his daily duties of delivering fresh bread and pastries to his customers scattered all over Paris.

His performance was, however, somewhat belittled by a controversy that ensued. It so, happened that the American entrant, Arthur Newton, from the halfway point onward was convinced that he was leading all the rest and none overtook him thereafter. At the finishing line, therefore, he was jubilant of his being the victor but was shocked to learn that he had finished a trailing fifth. This he could not believe, and to prove his point accused the ultimate winner, Frenchman Micheal Theato of having deviated from the prescribed path by taking short cuts and loop routes which was made possible because of his intimate knowledge of the zig-zag, meandering and confusing path through the streets of Paris. The argument, however, failed to elicit any support as a Swede, Ernst Fast, had also covered the distance half an hour earlier than Newton to claim the third spot. The marathon race of the 1900 Olympic Games, nevertheless, was a grueling affair, run under 102° Fahrenheit (39° Centigrade) in which only eight of the nineteen starters completed the distance.

As against the 285 athletes drawn from 13 countries that competed in the Olympic Games at Athens four years ago, a record number of 1066 athletes from 20 countries assembled in Paris for the healthy competitions. For the first time, female athletes figured in the Olympic Games and they participated in golf and tennis. The first woman to win an Olympic gold medal was tennis player Chariotte "Chattie" Cooper of Great Britain.

The games which were patronised in the Paris Olympic Games were: archery, bowling, croquet, cycling, fencing, gymnastics, polo, rowing, shooting, swimming, tennis, water polo, yachting and track and field events.

On Sunday, July 22, the Games came to a formal end. To mark the closing ceremony, the French officers offered a banquet to the guest athletes and much of the bitterness that had generated was forgotten.

13

ST. LOUIS 1904
Devoid of Foreign Challenge

In sharp contrast to the mismanagement and farcical show in Paris and the poor performances of the competitors there, the third Olympic Games in St. Louis were well organised and keenly contested. But this exhausts the plus points that the 1904 Games can boast of.

On the other side, the representation of countries was deplorably poor, reducing the meet to more or less an all American affair. The long distance in those pre-jet days, together with the comparatively larger expenses involved, severely restricted continental Europe's participation. France, which had hosted the previous Games did not send any team at all; nor did England, ranked next only to the USA. In track and field events, countries which somehow managed to find resources and ventured participation, sent in very small contingents. In the result, out of 625 athletes who represented 12 countries, as many as 533 came from the USA, the host country, including eight women all of whom were entered in the archery event. Foreign representation was so meagre that in some events the US athletes competed only amongst themselves. No wonder, therefore, that out of a total of 250 medals, the US had a lion's share of 209 medals.

Absence of foreign challenge manifested itself more pronouncedly in track and field results as the US athletes bagged

21 'firsts', 22 'seconds', and 21 'thirds' in the 23 events that were gone through. These spectacular achievements, however, were devoid of substance as an international triumph because of almost nil, or at best, a lukewarm foreign challenge. The two foreign athletes who thwarted a cent per cent gold haul by the USA were Canada's stocky Etienne Desmerteau, a Montreal policeman, who left his job because he would not get leave for participation in the Olympic Games, and won the 56 pound weight throw — now a defunct event and Thomas Kiely of Ireland who picked up 6036 points to win a gold in the decathlon of which all the ten events were held on the same day. Kiely was earlier lured to represent Great Britain with an offer of a free trip, but he refused, paid his own expenses and represented Ireland.

The blunder committed in Paris four years earlier was repeated in St. Louis. The Olympic Games were so timed as to synchronise with the run of the Louisiana Purchase Exposition, called the World's Fair, which was being held to celebrate the 100th anniversary of the inclusion of the state of Missouri in the American Union. Once again, the Games played a minor role and rated second to the bigger event. And as if this was not enough, the political climate of the world was also not very healthy with the Russia-Japanese war of 1904 raging and causing world wide concern and diverting attention even from the World's Fair. The Olympic Games which were being held only as an adjunct to the bigger event were, therefore, all the more relegated to the background.

The Games were originally scheduled to be held in Chicago but were subsequently given to the Louisiana Purchase Exposition of St. Louis. In the result, the Games could assume lesser importance than the exhibition itself. The semi-official report on the 1904 Olympics runs thus : "All sports, given under the auspices of the Exposition must bear the name Olympic," and under this banner were held all sorts of events such as interscholastic events open only to schoolboys from the state of Missouri, open handicaps for residents of Missouri, YMCA championships, and so on. It was, therefore, rather impossible to differentiate which of them were truly under the Olympic banner.

The Games opened on Monday, August 29 and continued through the week till Saturday, September 3. President Roosevelt presided over the opening ceremony and Alice Roosevelt, the first lady of the USA, was always around, to give away the prizes to the winners. But public response was poor with crowds nowhere near those seen at Athens. However, bitter rivalry amongst various clubs, whose members made up the US contingent generated keen competition and all the existing Olympic records in track and field events were shattered. The timings returned and marks made were so impressive and the Olympics pace so fierce that it was anybody's guess if it would have made any difference in the final outcome even if the foreign challenge had been fully represented.

Four athletes crowned themselves with glory by winning three events each — needless to mention that all of them belonged to the USA. Ray Ewry repeated his performance of Paris by winning all the three standing jumps, the long jump, high jump and the hop, step and jump. In the standing high jump, the second place was won by Joseph Stadler who thus became the first black athlete to win an Olympic medal in a field event. Archie Hahn reigned supreme in the short distance sprints and emerged as the fastest runner. He taped ahead of the great fields in the 60 metres, 100 metres and 200 metres dash. In the final of 200 metres, the other three challengers, Cartmell, Hogenson and Moulton, each false started once and according to the rules prevailing then they were penalised to take start from two yards behind the starting line. This gave Hahn a good initial leverage which he capitalised to his advantage by winning the race in the Olympic record time of 21.6 secs.

Harry L. Hillman of New York proved his excellence both in hurdles and flat races. He won in fine style the 200 and 400 metres hurdles and then outclassed all in the most hotly contested 400 metres flat race to join the ranks of the four triple winners of the Olympic Games in St. Louis. In this 400 metres event, fifteen contestants arrayed the starting line as there were no heats. A scorching pace was set from the very beginning as everybody made a bid for the lead in the inner lane. Groman of Chicago occupied the choice spot but as the runners entered the stretch, the curly haired, smiling Hillman galloped to the fore, hotly pursued, rather flanked by Waller and Poage upto the end. A final spurt of furious long strides and Hillman had breasted the tape first.

And then there was James D. Lightbody of Chicago who, on the opening day of the Games, skimmed over the hurdles and plunged in water-pits, in the fashion of a thoroughbred hunter, to win the 2,500 metre steeplechase against a strong challenge. Three days later, on Thursday, he won a great victory in what is regarded as the finest race of the 1904 Olympics, the 800 metres. In the company of such renowned names as George Underwood. Howard Velentine, John Runge and Breitkreutz on the starting line, Lightbody was not even in the reckoning. A sizzling pace was set right from the crack of the gun and true to expectations, Underwood and Breitkreutz shot in the lead with Runge and Valentine close on their heels. Soon Runge found the pace too fast to sustain any further and faded out but Lightbody was steadily narrowing the early lead he had conceded to his more reputed rivals. Until 100 metres from the finish, the race seemed to be among the first three in the lead but then Lightbody who was trailing fifth till then, put in a splendid burst of speed and galloped past runner after runner and 50 metres from the tape, he was the winner all the way.

Two days later, Lightbody wound up an exceptionally successful week when he won the gruelling 1,500 metres race in the Olympics record time of 4 minutes 5.4 seconds and thus also achieved the unique distinction of becoming a triple winner in the Olympic Games.

The discus throw event at the St. Louis Olympic Games of 1904 witnessed a tie for the first and only time in Olympic history. Both Martin Sheridan and Ralph Rose heaved the disc 128 ft. 10 ½ inches away. This necessitated a throw off for determining the first place. Both of them were given three throws in which Sheridan won by about five feet.

Another instance of a repeat performance was seen in the 50 yards swimming event, held in an ornamental lake where swimmers were required to take a start from a raft. This time the swim-off was necessitated owing to disagreement in the verdict of judges which roused tempers to fighting pitch. Zoltan Halmay of Hungary and J. Scott Leary of the USA both swam the 50 yds in the disputed time of 28.2 secs. In the swim-off, the Hungarian clocked 28.0 secs. which was 0.6 sec. faster than Leary's time of 28.6 secs.

The prestigious marathon race, true to tradition, provided thrills galore. It was won by T.J. Hicks in 3 hours, 28 minutes and 53 seconds.The race was run under scorching heat and only 14 out of the 31 runners completed the distance. The heat made worse by the dust stirred up by the accompanying autos, which were reminiscent of antique pieces, was too much of a hazard. Some of the runners collapsed midway; Bill Garcia of San Francisco being the worst sufferer. The winner, T.J. Hicks, an English born brass worker from Massachusetts, gained the lead around the halfway mark but was so exhausted that his further continuance was becoming a remote possibility. His handlers, Charles Lucas and Hugh McGarth, trotting along side, revived him with repeated doses of one-sixteeth grain of strychnine mixed with raw egg white, besides other stimulants (The use of drugs was later prohibited by the Olympic rules). Hicks plodded on, covered the last ten miles in a state of mental haze and encouraged by the bucking up of the crowd, tottered over the finishing line in a dazed condition. He collapsed thereafter and four doctors had to pool in their efforts to revive him.

Other highlights of the marathon race in St. Louis, viz., the antics of the pygmy Felix Carvajal, Fred Lorz, - the imposter, etc., have already been narrated in an earlier chapter captioned "The Marathon Story".

Although the Games passed off successfully, they could hardly retrieve the prestige of the Olympic movement which had received a grievous blow at Paris due to inept handling and mismanagement of the Games. At St. Louis, they were virtually sacrificed again at the altar of the World Fair and due to the participation of fewer countries, the ideal of the international character of the Games was in jeopardy. Some drastic action was needed to give a shot in the arm, and Coubertin was seized of the problem.

14

ATHENS 1906 (Unofficial) The Intercalated Games

Coubertin was sorely disappointed at the way the Games at Paris and St. Louis had tarnished the image and lowered the prestige of the Olympic Games. But he was not disheartened. Shrewed as he was, he found a way out by proposing to hold a mid-Olympic Games at Athens every four years, over and above the regular Olympics, to redeem the lost glory. This satisfied the Greek ego and insistence of making Athens the permanent venue without in any way softening Coubertin's firm resolve that the Games should be held in all corners of the world by rotation.

The mid-Olympic Games, however, could not be held a second time because of the mounting cost of organising the Games every four years coupled with the political unrest in Greece. For this reason, as also the purists' point of view that an Olympiad is of four years duration, the 1906 Games in Athens are treated as 'unofficial' although they were responsible to a very great extent in restoring the lost prestige and imparting permanency to the Olympic Games.

The grandeur and splendor, the milling crowds and the unbounded fervour and zest of the decade ago were once again on display. The capacity crowd of 60,000 and thousands more perched on the hills around, witnessed the opening ceremony on April 22, in which the royalty was not only fully represented but was seen engaged heart and soul in making the Games a grand success. The colourful royalty led by King George of Greece, who formally opened the Games, included Queen Alexandra of England, King Edward VII and Queen Olga of Greece. The Greek princes, George, Nicholas and Andrew, were the key officials supervising the Games assisted by crown prince Constantine, chairman-in-charge and chief referee of the Games. A fanfare of trumpets and an impressive march past by the athletes followed by display of Swedish exercises marked the opening ceremony. A truly international character was imparted to the Games by 901 competitors representing a record number of 21 nations.

Youthful Paul Pilgrim of the USA was the sensation of the 1906 Games. Strangely enough, he was not selected to make the USA team but scraped enough money to pay for his expenses and was there at Athens to participate in the Games. In the 400 metres race he was nowhere in the reckoning in the earlier stages of the exciting contest amidst such giants as Hillman, triple winner at St. Louis, Bacon and Moulton of USA, Wyndham Halswelle and Nigel Barker of Australia. But all of a sudden midway, Paul Pilgrim started springing full blast and, in a burst of speed, streaked past them to tape inches ahead in a thrilling finish.

His triumph in the 800 metres race followed the same pattern. Halswelle and RP Crabbe of England and Lightbody, the triple winner two years ago, were great names at the distance but Paul Pilgrim breasted the tape ahead of them all to join the ranks of Ray Ewry and MJ Sheridan who were the only other double winners in the track and field events of the 1906 Games.

Lightbody was the favourite for this event but he paid the penalty for his over confidence. Midway down the home stretch, he indulged in the luxury of looking back over his left shoulder to check the position of other contenders. Just then, Paul Pilgrim streaked past him from the right to breast the tape one tenth of a second earlier—Incidentally, Paul Pilgrim never won a major race before or after the 1906 Games.

The 1,500 metres walk was a new item added for the first time in the Olympic programme. George Bonhag of the USA, a long distance runner, having been disappointed at his performance in the five - mile race in which he finished fourth, entered the walking event in which he was an absolute novice. He was not conversant even with the rudiments of this event which required perfection in the technique of heel-and-toe work. In the brisk walking events it is often difficult to differentiate between walking and running and therefore the judges have an onerous responsibility and a difficult task to perform and are always subject to bitter criticism. Prince George was the chief judge and no sooner had the race begun than he started warning and disqualifying erring competitors. Since everyone wants to move the fastest, the chances of infringement of rules are the maximum. One by one, all the competing athletes were disqualified save George Bonhag who was shaking with laughter when he strolled over the finishing line in the fashion of a morning walker to win the championship in an event he was trying for the first time.

The disqualifications galore in the 1500 metre walk prompted the officials to stage a 3000 metre walking event also just by way of providing the disappointed participants another chance of showing their mettle. But this, too, did not make any difference and the story of a spate of disqualifications was repeated once again. For a change, however, this time it was an Hungarian, Gyorgy Sztancsis, who had the last laugh as he walked away with a 'gold' when all the leaders in the race defaulted.

Ray Ewry was once again unbeatable in his two standing jump events. The best all-round athlete, however, was Martin Sheridan of the USA who won the shot put event with a mighty throw of 40 feet 4 and 4/5 inches and heaved the discus 136 feet 1/3 inch away to earn the distinction of being a double winner. He followed it up with second places in 14-pound stone throw, the standing broad jump and the standing high jump.

The marathon race attracted 73 contestants, more than half of whom were Greeks, Fabulous prizes were promised to be awarded should a Greek won the prestigious race. The eventual winner, however, was the slim, short statured W. J. Sherring of Canada. Thus, all the tall offers and handsome prizes which smacked of chauvinism went abegging. Among the 73 starters, there was a 20-year old Italian, Dorando Pietri, who went unnoticed as he had to drop out due to some stomach trouble. But he was destined to become a living legend before the decade was out.

An interesting incident was witnessed in the weightlifting event. Josef Steinbach of Austria was accused of being a professional and had to retire following jeering and vocal outbursts against him. The field thus cleared, Tofolas, a Greek, won the event. While the prize distribution ceremony for the event was in progress, Steinbach entered the arena non-challantly and with effortless case lifted the weight which Tofolas had managed with all the grimaces on his face. Steinbach repeated this thrice, cast scornful glances at the spectators and withdrew.

The Americans once again asserted their all round superiority in the track and field events by winning 11 gold medals out of the 20.

Although labelled as the 'unofficial' Games, the 1906 meet in Athens was a turning point in the history of the Olympic Games as the uncertainties plagueing the future of the Games were removed once and for all.

Notwithstanding the tremendous boost that the 1906 Games in Athens provided to the Olympic movement, it has to be conceded that in the conduct and organisation of the games there was plenty of scope for improvement. The tracks were not only soft but had sharp turns with straights some 200 yards long. And to make matters worse the races were run in clockwise direction; conditions were thus not at all conducive for stern competitions. Track and field events apart, which incidentally included rope climbing and lifting the bar bell (one hand and both hands), the competitions in swimming were totally disorganised as confusion often prevailed about the commencement of the events. In the result, the competitors had to wait for hours which affected their performances. Charles Daniels of the USA who won two 'golds' at St. Louis in 1904 had to rest content with a very slow timing of 1 min. 3.0 secs for the 100 metres freestyle. Similarly, Otto Scheff of Austria in 400 metres (6 min. 23.8 sec) and Henry Taylor of Great Britain in 1600 metres (28 min. 28.0 secs.) freestyle returned timings well in excess of their best.

And then there was the much talked about and controvertial officiating in the fencing events. Out of the five fencing events, three went to France and one to Germany but in the Sabre (individual), the victory of the Greek, Jean Georgiadis, was subjected to vehement criticism. The officiating judge was accused of being partisan to his countryman but subsequent investigations revealed that as a matter of fact, he was ignorant of rules.

Notwithstanding the above shortcomings, the 1906 Games in Athens, known variously as the 'Intercalated' or 'Interim' Games gave a much needed shot-in-the arms to the Olympic movement after the disorganised competitions in Paris in 1900 and the unbecoming arrangements at St. Louis in 1904. More important, the 1906 Games imparted to the Olympics a touch and the form which has persisted ever since.

15

LONDON 1908
A Splendid Success

London was the makeshift venue after Rome, where the Games were originally scheduled to be held, had cried off giving no more than a year to the new venue for preparations. Lord Desborough, himself a fine sportsman, headed the newly organised British Olympic Committee which rose to the occasion and made excellent arrangements at such a short notice. A magnificient white city stadium, with a seating capacity of over 70,000, was built at Shepherds Bush in London. It was a multi-purpose stadium which, besides the cinder track, boasted of a 660 yard concrete cycling track, a 100 metre long swimming pool with a collapsible diving tower that could be removed from sight when not in use, and arrangements for wrestling events. Everything was spick and span and in perfect readiness for the great occasion on July 13, 1908 when King Edward VII, with Queen Alexandra by his side, formally signalled the Games open.

Despite meticulous planning and perfect arrangements, there were a few slips here and there, and with one slip leading to the other, discontent among athletes and officials mounted in geometrical progression. Thus, in the heat of competition, there raged a storm of protests and counter-protests giving rise to all sorts of misgivings against the organisers.

It all started with an innocuous controversy concerning national flags of competing nations. The new stadium was bedecked with colourful national flags but curiously enough, either inadvertently or by design, the flags of the USA and Sweden were conspicuous by their absence. The contingent from the USA took umbrage and retaliated immediately in a novel way; their standard bearer did not, against the customary practice, dip the stars and stripes while passing in front of the Tribune of Honour. The Swedes, on the other hand, did not express their resentment immediately but it found expression later in vehement protests against official rulings.

Then there were the Finns who marched flagless to register their disapproval of pressure tactics adopted by the Russians through diplomatic channels to make them compete under Russian banner. Likewise, the Irish temper flared up on learning that Ireland could compete only under the Union Jack.

These unfortunate incidents cast their shadow on the Games themselves; rains, often in torrents, rendered the atmosphere worse. As a matter of fact, inclement weather continued almost throughout the run of the Games.

On the opening day, only heats in the 400 and 1,500 metres were run. The following day, John J. Flanagan of USA repeated his performances of Paris and St. Louis by winning a gold medal in hammer throw and created a new Olympic record with a throw of 170 feet 4 1/16 inches. Melvin Sheppard (USA) won the 1,500 metres race in the record time of 4 minutes 3.4 seconds. The 'Peerless' Mel later won the 800 metres race also in an Olympic and world record time of 1 minute 52.8 seconds. This performance was matched by George Larner of Great Britain who won the 3,500 metres walking event on the second day, he later won the 10-mile walk race, too.

On the third day, the weather for once was fair but there was only one final on the card. Eric Lemming of Sweden threw the Javelin 178 feet 7 ¼ inches which was a neat 10 feet farther than the best attempt of Michel Dorizas of Greece who came in second. Lemming later hurled the javelin to a record distance of 179 feet 10 ⅝ inches in Greek style to earn his second 'gold'.

The weather reverted to its usual inclement self and the fourth day was wet as well as cold. Both the finals were almost swept by athletes from the USA. Martin Sheridan, who subsequently won the Greek style event also, set a record in the free style discus with a heave of 134 feet 1 13/16 inches. Ralph Rose was the other strong man who managed himself well on that slippery and heavy ground to put the weight farthest and win a gold for the USA.

The Games so far were going on rather smoothly, the volley of protests and accusations notwithstanding. The reason was that while the aggrieved parties lodged protests against apparent injustice done to them, they never for a moment thought of assigning motives to the officials concerned. In the result, the protests so far lacked sting. But worst was to come. The row that was kicked up in the tug-of-war event on the fifth day was certainly none of the innocent variety.

Great Britain fielded several teams in the tug-of-war event. Liverpool Police, representing Great Britain 'B', was pitched against the USA. The rules of the event allow only ordinary walking shoes to be worn by the contestants. The Liverpoor Police, however, turned up in "monstrous boots", which was vehemently objected to by the USA team. The British officials turned down the protest justifying the footgear used by the Liverpool Police on the grounds that it was the "ordinary footwear" for the cops as they wore the kind of boots in the discharge of their daily duties. For the USA team, which had not even an outside chance with the opposition having such a tremendous foothold, the decision of the officials was downright partisan, favouring the home team with undue advantage in a bid to deprive the USA of the laurels. Consequently, in protest it gave way at the first try but the explanation given for its withdrawal by the British officials was "because they had enough of it" which added insult to injury for the USA contingent.

The protests which were hitherto lodged in a subdued tone, now erupted into vociferous outbursts of slanderous allegations. The spokesmen of the USA contingent had already protested against the entry of Tom Longboat, a Canadian, in the marathon race who had been dubbed as professional in the USA. They were now pointing out irregularities committed in diverse ways — in dividing the lot for the trial heats, the British athletes being assisted and instructed by the officials judging the contests, the rough treatment meted out to the members of the American Olympic Committee in not allowing them on the field while the competitions were in progress, the arbitrary fashion in which their genuine protests were being summarily rejected.

The most eventful day, however, was Thursday, July 24, when one of the bitterest controversies was sparked off. On the marks of the 400 metres final race were the three Americans. Carpenter, Robbins and Taylor pitched against the lone British representative and the hot favourite, Wyndham Halswelle. The newspapers had a field day in speculating and debating the prospects in the race which had only helped in stirring up national prejudices.

Taylor was slow in taking off and soon faded out. But the remaining three ran neck and neck until they entered the stretch when Carpenter shot into the lead. Suddenly, some one from amongst the British officials yelled 'foul' and an over-enthusiastic official rushed in and snipped the tape at the finish before Carpenter, Robbins and Halswelle dashed in that order. The British officials hastened to explain to a bewildered group of US athletes that Carpenter had blocked and cut in front of Halswelle on the turn. Carpenter was therefore, disqualified and the race ordered to be re-run. The USA contingent went mad with rage and damning and swearing at all and sundry withdrew the remaining two athletes from the race. In consequence, on the final day, Halswelle ran the distance all alone and thus earned a "walkover" victory which, perhaps, is unique in the annals of track and field events of the Olympic Games.

On Friday, July 25, the great marathon race featuring the "Dorondo" affair was run, which has already been narrated in sufficient detail in an earlier chapter. The Italians were furious over the way the British officials handled their star runner Pietri Dorondo and disqualified him. Their grouse was that it was the muddling interference of the British officials which was responsible for the disqualification of their hero otherwise Pietri Dorondo would have won the race on his own if left alone.

While there was plenty of furore about so many different incidents, the performance of the British officials deserved to be judged more charitably. After all, they had undertaken a stupendous task and shouldered onerous responsibilities at a short notice.

A more charitable view should have been taken of their short-comings which were bound to occur due to sheer inexperience. And then, it has to be conceded that in such circumstances, minor incidents and mishaps are quite often blown out of all proportions. At any rate, after the London Olympics, the International Olympic Committee made drastic and radical changes in the rules for the conduct of the Games. The overall supervision and management of every particular sport was thenceforth vested in the respective international governing bodies, with the host nation having no say in the matter.

In the midst of a plethora of protests and allegations some notable performances often received far less attention than they otherwise deserved. R E Walker, a 19 year-old schoolboy from South Africa, displayed superb sprinting powers to set up a record timing of 10.8 seconds in the 100 metres dash. He was given a standing ovation and was carried shoulder high to the dressing room by his enthusiastic supporters.

Interestingly, Walker was not originally selected for his country but was included only as an after thought.

Ray Ewry, in the fourth consecutive Olympics (counting the 1906 Games also), had yet to come across a rival to challenge his supremacy in the two events monopolised by him – the standing high jump and long jump. With his tally of 10 gold medals in the Olympic Games, he carved for himself a niche in the Temple of Fame.

In the pole vault event, Edward Cooke and Albert Gilbert, both of USA, created a record by clearing 12 feet 2 1/16 inches and were declared the joint winners, but not before a controversy regarding the "holes" or "well" for the pole and the "soft landing pit" was hotly contested.

Other athletes who established records in their specialities, all of whom incidentally from the USA, were John Hayes who covered the marathon distance in 3 hours 55 minute, 18.4 seconds; Forrest Smithson winning the 110 metres hurdles in 15 seconds dead. Charles Bacon, the noted middle distance hurdler, who covered the 400 metre hurdles in 55 seconds, Harry Porter leaping high enough in the running high jump to clear 6 feet, 2 $\frac{13}{16}$ inches, and Francis Iron clearing 24 feet 6 ½ inches in the running long jump. Timothy Ahearne was the only athlete from Great Britain to have established a record in the track and field events on the home ground. He covered 48 feet 11 $\frac{3}{8}$ inches in the triple jump event.

The unmerciful weather and the frayed tempers apart, the London Games of 1908, were a splendid success, on the whole, with 22 nations sending in a record number of 2,666 athletes it was a truly international meet held in a stately stadium where crowds braved the rains and rough weather in order not to miss the thrills of the Olympic Games.

16

STOCKHOLM 1912
Well Organised Games

Stockholm was awarded the Olympic Games in recognition of Sweden's constant and enthusiastic support to the Olympic Movement right from the very beginning. And appropriately enough, the Swedes lived up to the expectations and fully justified the trust reposed in them. The Games were superbly organised and all those who participated in, or witnessed the games, were unanimous in their ful-some praise that the Stockholm Games were by far the best staged till then.

The Swedes built a new double-deck stadium which remained filled with capacity crowds throughout the run of the Games. Royal patronage was available in ample measure which imparted grace, glamour and grandeur to the great show. Technical excellence was achieved through the skill and untiring efforts of J.E. Edstrom. An electrical timing device accurate to a tenth of a second was used for the first time for recording athletics performance with precision. The photo-finish cameras, an innovation, proved of utmost utility particularly in athletic performances in which keen competitions were witnessed. And then there was an elaborate network of public address system, besides informative charts, score boards and other devices which kept the spectators well informed.

Arrangements par excellence helped the athletes to be on their mettle. In the result, a record number of nineteen Olympic records were established. The Americans held sway in the track and field events as usual but some new nations made their mark also, and Sweden, the host country, had the distinction of winning the over all championship. The Finns, hitherto an absolute non-entity in the Olympic Games, gave a glimpse of what was up their sleeves for exhibition in a big way in the future Olympic Games. They bagged six gold medals which included three in the long distance races and three in throwing events.

King Gustaf V of Sweden inaugurated the Games on Saturday, July 6, amidst blowing of trumpets from the four towers of the new stadium, followed by an impressive march past resplendent with pomp and show. The glittering ceremony over, tracks were cleared in circus-like swiftness and trial heats of various races were run. The tone and temper of the keen competitions ahead was soon evident when in the fifth heats of the 100 metres races, Lippincott of USA sprinted the distance in the record time of 10.6 seconds.

In the finals of this short distance dash the following day, there were seven false starts in one of which Ralph Craig and Lippincott dashed down the full course. This gratuitous warming up apparently did them good as Craig ultimately won the race by breasting the tape 2 feet ahead of his nearest rival Alvah Meyer. Donald Lippincott got the third spot, a mere 6 inches behind Meyer to make the event a clean sweep for the USA. Ralph Craig later achieved the sprinting 'double' when he won the 200 metres spurt also against Lippincott in 21.7 seconds.

The same day, i.e. Sunday, July 7, saw the emergence of the greatest sporting star of the track and field history whose name, however, unfortunately does not find a place in the record books. That was the great Jim Thorpe, whose tribal name 'Bright Path' seemed to be appropriate as the athletic path that be tread was really bright. In an almost super-human display of all round athletic prowess, Jim swept the pentathlon event so overwhelmingly that the points scored by him were double those of his nearest rival, Ferdinand Bie. Of the five events, he was first in four of them, the 200 metres dash, the 1,500 metre run, the broad jump and the discus throw.

Later Jim Thorpe went on to win the decathlon event as well, this also, with a wide margin, and thus achieved the unique distinction of winning both the pentathlon and decathlon events in the same Olympic Games. After the 1924 Olympic Games the pentathlon event has been discontinued and as such the 'double' cannot be repeated by any one.

Decathlon was introduced for the first time in Stockholm and it has since continued as a regular item on the Olympic programme. An almost similar event with the nomenclature 'All round championship' was held in the 1904 Olympic Games but was discontinued thereafter. Decathlon consists of ten events, namely, 100 metres dash, long jump, 400 metres flat, discus throw, pole vault, javelin throw, shotput, 110 metres hurdles, high jump and 1,500 metre run.

Jim Thorpe was undoubtedly the shinning star of the 1912 Games but the radiance of the Bright Path faded and dimmed when long after the conclusion of the Games a Boston newspaper published a revealing story accusing Jim Thorpe of having violated the code of amateurism when he accepted money for playing base ball in a semi pro-league in North Carolina in 1910. Jim confessed with utter frankness: "I hope I will be partly excused by the fact that I was simply an Indian schoolboy and did not know I was doing wrong… I was not very wise to the ways of the world."

Olympic rules do not permit professionalism and there could not be an exemption for the renowned athletic genius. His prizes were reclaimed and awarded to Ferdinand Bie of Norway (Pentathlon) and Hugo Wieslander of Sweden (Decathlon), runners-up in the two events.

On the third day, i.e., Monday, July 8, another all-time great star burst on the horizon – Hannes Kolehmainen, the first of the 'flying' Finns and a forerunner to a chain of distinguished athletes from Finland who were to be the star performers in the future Olympic Games. Hannes, the 'Mighty' was doubtless a prodigy who had no match in long distance races. He was a slim, 6 feet 6 inches tall, loose-limbed runner who with long, elegant and effortless strides astounded the athletic world by winning three gold medals in the 5,000 metres, 10,000 metres and 8,000 metres cross-country races. In the 10,000 metres which he covered in the Olympic and world record time of 31 minutes 20.8 seconds he beat his nearest rival, Lewis Tewanina of USA. by 46 seconds. Winning the 5,000 metres race, however, was not that easy and even though Hannes traversed this distance also in an Olympic and world record time of 14 minutes 36.6 seconds, he was hotly pursued, and at times even led by the French distant runner, Jean Bouin, who was only a stride behind at the finishing line with an equally astonishing timing of 14 minutes 36.7 seconds.

Paradoxically, Hannes Kolehmainen's best performance was in another event which he did not win after all. In the first heat of the 3,000 metres team race, Finland was pitted against the USA. It was a five man team event and Hannes ran his lap in a record time but his other team mates fared so badly that his team was eliminated despite his own splendid performance. USA, ultimately won this event against Sweden and Great Britain the next day, and Hannes suffered the mortification of seeing Tel Berna, whom he had beaten hollow the previous day, crossing the finishing line triumphantly.

There were exceptionally keen competitions in the three middle distance races – the 400 metres, 800 metres and 1,500 metres. Not only were new records established in each of these races, but the difference of timings of the winners and those at places was only of split seconds and the judges were often forced to await the results of the photo finish cameras before declaring the winner. In the 800 metres, which the young sensation, James Meredith won in Olympic and world record time of 1 minute 51.9 seconds against a great field, the second and third places went to Melvin Sheppard and Ira Davenport, respectively, both of whom returned the identical time of 1 minute 52 seconds which was only one-tenth of a second less than the winner. The fact that all of them broke the world record coupled with the astounding fact that the next three runners also broke the existing Olympic record time of 1 minute 52.8 seconds speaks volumes of the sizzling pace set by the runners in this historic race.

Similarly, in the 1,500 metres race, the record time of 3 minutes 56.8 seconds clocked by Arnold Jackson of Great Britain was barely one-tenth of a second faster than the Americans Abel Kiviat and Norman Taber who finished second and third in the same time of 3 minutes 56.9 seconds. The pace in this race also was so fast that all the first five runners broke the existing record of 4 minutes 3.4 seconds set by Melvin Sheppard four years ago by more than five seconds.

Another great race was the 400 metres which after three false starts was won by Charles Reidpath when he left the field behind in one of his characteristic whirlwind rushes down the stretch to breast the tape ahead of Hans Braun of Germany and fellow-American Edward Lindberg in an Olympic and world record time of 48.2 seconds. For the first time, the Swedes had hit upon the idea of using separate lanes for the 400 metres race to avoid recurrence of 'Halswelle' type incident of the 1908 Olympic Games in London.

The course for the marathon race run on Sunday, July 14 was from the stadium to the village of Solentuna and back.

The distance was 40,200 metres and the 68 starters had to endure the twin ordeals of excessive heat and dusty steep hills. Francisco Lazaro of Portugal, could not withstand the strain and the gruelling heat. After 19 miles of plodding he collapsed, was carried to the hospital where he died the following day. Kenneth McArthur of South Africa won in the record time of 2 hours 36 minutes 54.8 seconds with Christoper Gitsham also of South Africa second and Gaston Strobine of the USA third.

Trial in endurance and stamina reminds the final wrestling bout (Greco-Roman style) in the middle weight 'B' class in which the Swede Anders Ahlgren and the Finn Ivar Bohling grappled for six hours at a stretch without reaching a decision. The fight was declared a dead heat and both the wrestlers were awarded silver medals.

The running high jump event is memorable not only for the record leap of 6 feet 3-15/16 inches by Almer Richards of the USA but also for the introduction of a new style known as the

"Californian roll" which soon replaced the traditional 'scissor' style. American George Horine was the innovator who although finishing third, had played a pioneering role.

The Swedes introduced a new event and entitled it 'Modern Pentathlon' which has since been a regular item on the Olympic programme. The event comprises competitions in five disciplines – shooting (pistol, from a 25 metre range), swimming (300 metres free style), fencing (epee), riding (800 metres course with 15 obstacles) and cross-country race of 4,000 metres. Appropriately, as also understandably, the Swedes swept this event with Gustaf Lillienhook winning the gold medal.

The Swedes also introduced art contests in which prizes were awarded for masterpieces in architecture, literature, music, painting and sculpture. The literature prize was ostensibly shared by two Germans: George Hohrod and M.Eschbach but these in effect were pseudonyms; the real author of the winning poem captioned "Ode to Sport" was the great Coubertin himself who symbolically chose German names to typify the Olympic spirit which aims at creating rapprochement between conflicting nations.

In the list of many 'firsts' for which the Olympic Games of 1912 are fondly remembered, were the swimming events opened to women for the first time. Competitions in three events : 100 metres free-style, high diving and 4 × 100 metres relay, were held exclusively for women which were won by Fanny Durack of Australia, Greta Johansson of Sweden and the foursome Bella Moore, Irena Steer, Annie Speira and Jennie Fletcher of Great Britain, respectively. In the men's 100 metres free-style swimming event, Duke Paoa Kahanamoku of the USA exhibited for the first time the 'flutter-kick' and the 'crawl' strokes with telling effect.

Judged by any standard and with whatever yardsticks applied, the Olympic Games in Stockholm were by far the best organised till then. Twenty-eight nations, drawn from all the five continents of the globe, sent in 2,541 athletes including 57 women and imparted the great assembly a truly international character. The royal reception, the regal hospitality and the hearty send-off were cherished by the athletes and officials for long and the great show fostered international amity and goodwill. The Olympic movement had matured and the tender sapling which had been planted at Athens in 1896 had come to full bloom at Stockholm and not even the conflagration of the First World War could scorch it.

17

ANTWERP 1920
Emergence of Finns

The regular sequence of the Olympic Games was interrupted when the VIth Olympiad scheduled to be held in Berlin in 1916, had to be cancelled due to the First World War. The Olympic spirit, however, came out unscatched through the holocaust and as soon as the guns were silenced and peace dawned, plans for holding the next Olympic Games were taken in hand.

The choice for the 1920 Games fell on Antwerp although war-swept Belgium was still reeling under the devastating effects of four years of occupation by the enemy. Undeterred by the crippled resources and the aftermath of war, the tiny country girded up its loin and bent its energies to the great, stupendous task of playing host to the grand event at short notice. A stadium was built in hardly a year's time. True, the turf and the cinder path for staging the track and field competitions were not upto the mark but no efforts were spared and whatever was humanly possible was done. It redounds to the credit of a small country, laid waste by war, to have done so much at such short notice.

Before the Games were declared open formally, a mass religious service, led by Cardinal Mercler, was held in the imposing Cathedral of Antwerp, in memory of the athletes killed in the World War.

On Saturday, August 14, a refreshing spectacle greeted the beholders - a splash of colour provided by the multi-coloured uniforms of 2,606 athletes, representing 29 countries, as they paraded in the new stadium for the opening ceremony which was formally performed by King Albert of Belgium. For the first time thousands of pigeons, symbolic of peace and goodwill, were released to herald the opening of the Games. This practice has since become a regular feature, forming part and parcel of the opening ceremony.

But this was not the only innovation to have been introduced by the Belgians and taken in the Olympic fold. For the first time also, the Olympic oath on behalf of the participants was taken; the honour fell on Victor Boin, a member of the Belgium Fencing team which was placed second in the Epee team event. With his right hand raised he delivered the oath in clear, ringing tone: "In the name of all competitors, I promise that we will take part in these Olympic Games, respecting and abiding by the rules which govern them, in the true spirit of sportsmanship, for the glory of sport and the honour of our teams."

It was also at Antwerp that the Olympic emblem, with its five interlaced rings, made its appearance for the first time in the Olympic Games. Ice hockey as an Olympic event was also introduced for the first time.

The Antwerp Games were singularly different from all the preceding ones on more than one count. Till then, the champion nations (unofficial, though) had always been the host country: Greece in 1896 in Athens. France in 1900 in Paris, USA in St. Louis in 1904, Great Britain 1908 in London and Sweden in 1912 in Stockholm. But in Antwerp, Belgium finished fifth with only 41 medals out of the 438. And then, the continued dominance of the track and field events by the USA received a rude jolt when their superiority was severely challenged by athletes from Finland. The Finns won nine gold medals in track and field, the same number as the US, although Finland had fielded only 30 competitors as against 101 by the USA. Another notable feature was the ascendancy of the newcomers which was evident from the fact that there were only three double winners at Antwerp and not one of them wore the Stars and Stripes shield. At Stockholm, it was Hannes the Mighty who stole the limelight; at Antwerp, the Pearless Paavo cornered the glory.

Morning shows the day may be a trite expression but often proves a point. The first event finalised at Antwerp was the javelin throw and the first four, who were all Finns, bettered the Olympic and world record – Jonni Myrre winning the 'gold' with a record throw of 215 feet 9 ½ inches. Incidentally, it was the first occasion in the annals of modern Olympics that such a feat was accomplished by a nation other than the USA and was a sure pointer of the nature of contests that were to follow.

The next day, the USA responded with a clean sweep of the 400 metres hurdles, Frank Loomis establishing an Olympic and world record of 54 seconds dead with team mates John Norton and August Desch taking the second and third places respectively. Another sweep for the USA was in the 100 metres dash in which the hot favourite Charles Paddock led all the rest with a timing of 10.8 seconds. Paddock later won a silver medal in the 200 metres dash behind Allen Woodring. Paddock is, however, known more for the technique that he developed in finishing his races with a 10 feet leap. Experts often doubted if his finishing leaps were of any advantage but his successes in his specialities were there to prove the efficacy of his novelty.

Mention of 200 metres race recalls the comedy when the apparent handicap and panic which gripped Allen Woodring before the commencement of the races ultimately turned out to be a boon in disguise for him in winning the event.

Having fared none too well in the official trials at home, Woodring was included in the USA Olympic squad only on second thoughts. On arrival in Antwerp, however, he set for himself so rigorous a training schedule that his sprinting shoes gave way and were worn out beyond repair. Left with no alternative, he had to borrow a pair which incidentally had unusually long spikes. Paucity of time did not permit filing down the spikes to length and Woodring was on the starting block in great trepidation. The extra length of the spikes, however, afforded the precise foothold on that damp and heavy track and lo and behold, he won the Olympic event in borrowed shoes.

But as at Stockholm eight years ago, the long distance races were the centre of attraction, at Antwerp, too. And if Hannes Kolehmainen was the hero who held aloft his country's banner in the last Olympics, here was an athletic prodigy in the person of Paavo Nurmi who emerged and blossomed out at Antwerp to reign supreme in long distance races at three successive Olympic Games, bringing home to the world the athletic prowess of his sparcely populated country – Finland.

Nurmi's debut in the 5,000 metre run at Antwerp could not be termed sensational. But the connoisseurs of athletic ability were quick to spot the phenomenal youngster and knew that a 'sensation' had risen on the horizon. Nurmi came second best in this race yielding to the French war veteran Joseph Guilemot, but not before matching him stride by stride and leading most of the time. Guillemot was a veteran of many races and enjoyed immense popularity and sympathy; firstly, because he was a victim of war having been badly gassed on the 'front' thus damaging his lungs and then he was endowed with a very affable and jovial nature, which won him countless friends. Trailing behind Nurmi at the start of the final stretch, he suddenly launched a fantastic spurt and shot past to win in 14 minutes 35 seconds – a neat ten yards ahead of Nurmi.

Three days later Guillemot and Nurmi were once again locked in a grim tussle for supremacy, this time in double the earlier distance, i.e., 10,000 metres race. Nurmi, having profited by the experience gained in the earlier reverse, let the Frenchman set the pace this time only to dazzle him with a burst of speed in the last stretch to win gold in 31 minutes 45.8 seconds – the first of his nine Olympic gold medals.

The two great adversaries were pitted against each other a third time in the 10,000 metres cross-country and with one victory to each against the other, excitement was at its pitch. But there was an anti-climax as Guillemot accidentally stumbled on some highly uneven surface along the way, fell down and had to abandon the race. With no threat of any serious challenge Nurmi won the race in 27 min. 15 sec. with Erik Backman of Sweden close on heel and fellow countryman Heikki Llimatainen 22 secs behind. The timings, however, were too good to be true. The course was, therefore, re-measured and was found to be considerably less than 10,000 metres.

Later Nurmi, teaming with Liimtainen and Koskeniemi bagged gold medal for Finland in the 10,000 metres cross-country team competition. Great Britain and Sweden were placed second and third respectively.

Two other athletes distinguished themselves by becoming double winners at Antwerp. For Albert George Hill of Great Britain, it was a marvelous feat to win both the 800 metres and the 1,500 metres races – a record that could not be equalled in the next 44 years until Peter Snell of New Zealand did it in Tokyo in 1964. To think that Hill was past his prime when he achieved this distinction at the age of 36….!

The other 'double winner' was Italy's Ugo Frigerio, the merry maestro who 'walked away' with both the walking events of 3,000 and 10,000 metres. Long distance walking events lack glamour and are often downright boring with no spectator appeal whatsoever but Ugo had plenty of antics to wheedle the public and rivet their attention in following the progress of the events.

The track, prepared none too well and, to make matter worse, rendered soggy by the rains that poured often, was far from being ideal for bringing out the best in the competitions. Still, eight Olympic and four world records were created in the track and field events. Earl Thompson of Canada clocked 14.8 secs. in 110 metres hurdles and Frank Loomis of the USA did the 400 metres hurdles in 54 secs. dead to establish world records.

The javelin throw event was a clean sweep for Finland. The remarkable thing about this event was that the first five place winners – of whom the first four were Finns – all improved upon the Olympic and world record of 198 feet 11 ⅜ inches. Jonni Myrra won the gold medal with his record throw of 215 feet 9 ¾ inches.

The fourth world record was established in the 4 x 100 metres relay won in 42.2 secs. by the USA quartet of Paddock, Scholx, Murchison and Kirkse.

Hannes Kolehmainen, the hero of the 1912 Olympic Games, in his farewell appearance won the traditionally prestigious marathon race in the Olympic record time of 3 hrs. 32 mins. 35.8 secs.

Despite their superiority in the track and field events having been seriously challenged by Finland and Great Britain, the USA had the distinction of securing the overall championship (unofficial). The loss of supremacy in the track and field events was amply compensated by sweeping victories in Shooting, Swimming, Rowing and Boxing.

The efficient handling of the Games by the war ravaged Belgium was highly commendable even though public response was not the least encouraging. The stadium with a seating capacity of over 30,000 used to be thinly occupied by the spectators although the 30 cents entrance fee was fairly low for such a big global affair. The authorities even made the entrance free and the schools and colleges were persuaded to come enbloc in an effort to project a sporting image of the Belgians whose minds were still in a daze and their souls still shaken with the shocks of the war to think of any recreational pastime.

18

PARIS 1924
Lost Honour Redeemed

Coubertin ardently wished Paris to be the venue of the Olympic Games in 1924 to commemorate the 30th anniversary of its rebirth. The idea to revive the Olympic Games was mooted in June 1894. But Amsterdam had better claims as it was a candidate since 1916, and in 1920 had voluntarily withdrawn in favour of Antwerp. Claims apart, once again the Dutch showed their magnanimity and in deference to the desires of the founder of the modern Olympic Games, whom they held in the highest esteem, bowed out.

The eighth Olympiad in Paris presented a sharp contrast to the fiasco of 1900 – the last time when Paris managed – or mismanaged – the Olympic Games. The French government was fully determined this time to redeem its honour in the world of sports; it left no stones unturned in this behalf and the games were a grand success.

The newly created Colombes stadium was packed to capacity, as it remained throughout the run of the Games, to witness the impressive opening ceremony on Saturday, July 5. A record number of 3,092 athletes (including 136 women) representing 44 nations marched past the royal-box filled with dignitaries from home and abroad. French President Gaston Doumergue, surrounded by the then Prince of Wales, Crown Princes of Sweden and Rumania, Regent of Abyssinia, a host of ambassadors and other notables, declared the Games open and administered the Olympic oath to

George Andre, a French hurdler representing all the participating athletes by proxy. The full programme of the opening ceremony took the whole afternoon so that the competitions could commence only the next day, Sunday, July 6.

The record breaking spree, which was the highlight of the 1924 Olympic Games, started right from the first event on the card. Vile Ritola of Finland, who undoubtedly would have enjoyed much greater eminence if only he had not been a contemporary of Nurmi, astounded the athletic world by running the 10,000 metres in a world record time of 30 minutes, 23.2 secs, and that too, on a track rendered heavy by rains in the morning. This incredible feat bettered the previous record by more than 12 secs. And it was therefore, no surprise if Edvin Wide of Sweden who won the silver medal was as much as 27 seconds behind Ritola. Jonny Myrra also of Finland, who had created a record at Antwerp in javelin throw, had not to exert much to win this item which was the only other event finalised on that day.

Monday, July 7, not only saw competitors making a mincemeat of previous records but also witnessed some memorable events. Eero Lehtonen of Finland won the pentathlon event with Elemer Somfay of Hungary coming second. But it was Robert DeGendre of the USA who, even though placed third, stole the limelight. In the long jump, part of the pentathlon programme, LeGendre leapt a distance of 22 ft.8-7/16 inches and created a world record. Curiously enough, LeGendre had not entered in the Olympic long jump event in which USA's official entrants were Hart de Hubbard and Edward Gourdin, both Negroes, who had earned the first two places. It is said that there was no love lost between the official entrants and DeGendre who had declared even before his record breaking leap that he would prove his superiority over his rival team-mates in no uncertain manner.

In the 400 metre hurdles race, there was another eventful performance. Morgan Taylor of the USA was topping the timbers fast enough but tipped one of the hurdles before breasting the tape first. The default, however, deprived him of the honour of holding the official record although the fast time of 52.6 secs., returned by

Taylor remained the world's best for eight years until Robert Tisdall clipped it by 0.8 sec. in 1932.

In the 100 metres sprint, the fleet footed USA quartet, Peddock, Scholz, Murchison and Gowman, who had waded through a record number of 97 contestants from 35 nations, were hot favourites, with Porritt of New Zealand and Englishman Harold Abrahams treated as rank outsiders. But Abrahams proved to be the dark horse when he upset all calculations by streaking past the pack like a flash to establish a new record of 10.6 secs. Jackson Scholz was five feet behind and Arthur Porritt finished third. However, it was the bespectacled Harold Osborn who redeemed the prestige of the USA when he made a record leap of 6 feet 6 inches to win the high jump event.

The shot put item on the third day was a clean sweep for the USA with Glarence Houser putting away the weight farthest. But it was the 800 metres race which was significant and evoked interest not only because it was keenly contested but also because a new nation figured for the first time among the winners. Dr. Paul Martin of Switzerland, then a medical student but later a renowned bone specialist, was only a fraction of a second behind Douglas Lowe of Great Britain who was at the tape in 1 min. 52.4 secs.

Two great races were run on the fourth day, in both of which new records were established. The first was the 200 metres sprint in which all the six finalists were so renowned that no one was prepared to hazard a guess about the actual winner. And, of course, there was not a gasp of breath when, Harold Abraham, who had won the 100 metres in a record time only two days back, finished last in the race which was won and lost by hair's breadth. Scholz whizzed past a stunned Paddock right at the tape to match the world record of 21.6 secs. set by Lippincott in one of the heats at Stockholm.

The second record shattering performance of the day was dished out by Ville Ritola of Finland in the 3,000 metres steeple chase. In a fantastic display of skill and stamina in crossing hurdles and jumping in water pits he slashed the existing record by more than 26 seconds to return a timing of 9 min. 33.6 secs. Elias Katz, another Finn, who ran in second was no less than 60 metres behind.

Thursday, July 10, was the historic day when the "Peerless Paavo" astounded and entranced the athletic community by displaying incredible running ability. Within a span of a bare two hours he not only won two long distance races, the 1,500 metres and the 5,000 metres, but also established Olympic records in both. In the 1,500 metres he pared the existing record of Arnold Jackson by 3.2 secs. and although Willy Scharer of Switzerland and Honry Stallard of Britain, who ran second and third respectively, also broke the record, neither of them was anywhere near Nurmi. In the 5,000 metres, however, Ville Ritola was close on heels throughout and was only one-fifth of a second behind Nurmi whose record breaking timing of 14 min. 31.2 secs. was a full five seconds faster than Hannas Kitehmainen's performance of 1912.

Nurmi's signal achievements on that fifth day of competitions so over shadowed the days proceedings that Lee Barnes' and Glona Graham's record-breaking efforts in pole vault were totally eclipsed although these performances on any other day would have hit the headlines. As a matter of fact, seldom has such keen contest been witnessed as in the pole vault event of 1924. Both Barnes and Grahmm cleared 12 ft. 11 ½ inches equaling Harry Babcocks' record of 1912 but Barnes clinched the issue in the jump off. Likewise, James Brooker got into the third spot in a jump off after tying with a Dane at the height of 12 ft. 9-9/16 inches to make it a clean sweep for the USA.

Some stunning upsets were in store for the 400 metres event which was decided on Friday, July 11. The existing record for the distance was 48.2 secs. set by Charles Reidpath at Stockholm in 1912. This record was surpassed thrice in 24 hours. While, on the afternoon of July 10, Imbach of Switzerland had run in 48 secs. flat in one of the qualifying heats, the next morning, it was further improved when Horatio Fitch of the USA clocked 47.8 secs. A battle royal was thus anticipated in the final between these two record breakers, but the race was destined for a bizarre finale. A rank outsider who could never run the 400 metres in less than 49 secs, and as such not a competitor for this race originally, startled all and sundry by beating hollow all the big names with a record time of 47.6 secs, which remained unbeaten for the next eight years. He was none else than Reverend Eric Liddel, born in China and studied in Scotland, who was representing Great Britain and whose favourite event, in which he had any chance, was the 100 metres. But the short sprint was run on sabbath day and Reverend Eric was not one of those who would sacrifice their religious beliefs at the altar of mundane matters. He, therefore, entered the 400 metres event instead and the happy result apparently under divine dispensation, must have further strengthened his religious beliefs.

Excitement over Nurmi's performances of Thursday had hardly subsided when he was again on the starting mark on Saturday for 10,000 metre cross-country run. The day was extremely hot and of the 39 starters, 24 abandoned their efforts, succumbing to exhaustion and stress and strain of the enervating heat. A couple of them who obstinately strived to brave the ordeal landed themselves in trouble. One runner tottered into the stadium utterly dazed, lost his sense of direction, collided against a concrete wall, suffering grievous injuries in the bargain; the other, Spain's Andia Aguilar was the victim of a terrible sunstroke, which necessitated hospitalisation for several days. It was under these adverse conditions that Peerless Paavo ran a winner far ahead of all the rest with plenty of steam still left in him.

Besides the three gold medals in the individual events, the Ace of Abu (Abu is the name of Nurmi's native place) helped to win two more for his country in the 3,000 metre and 10,000 metre cross-country team competitions. Thus, in four days, the famous Flying Finn had bagged five gold medals, but with a veritable super-human one eventually ceases to marvel at his achievements.

On the last day of the track and field competitions there was virtually a crowd on the starting line of the marathon race. Fifty-eight runners from 19 nations were flagged from the Colombes stadium for Pontoise and back, for that was the course set — a distance of 42,195 metres. Steenroos, a wrestler turned runner, and a veteran at the age of 40 who had also competed at Stockholm 12 years back, ran the distance in 2 hours 41 min. 22.6 secs., a full

6 minutes ahead of his nearest challenger Roberto Bertini of Italy. Of course, it is needless to say that Steenroos was from Finland, but even for a Finn it was a remarkable triumph in the face of distressingly hot weather that the race was run and in view of the break in his running carrier consequent upon a leg fracture that he had sustained in the cross-country race some years back.

The 1924 Games are memorable for another superhuman performer, of course, not on terra firma where Nurmi reigned supreme, but in the pleasantly cool waters of the swimming pool. It was American Johny Weissmuller who shattered records in the 100 metres and 400 metres free-style events. He was the anchor man on the record breaking, victorious relay team and also had a big share in earning a bronze medal for his country's water polo team. In the 100 metres, Weismuller's record time of 59 seconds flat was a good 6 secs better than the 16 years old record set by Charles Daniels in London, and in the 400 metres he eclipsed the pre-war record by a full 20 secs. Four years later, Weismuller improved his own record of 100 metres in Amsterdam before entering filmdom to enthrall a wider audience as Tarzan of the screens.

Mention of films brings to mind other prospective cine stars who first performed only as athletes in the Olympic Games in Paris. Hollywood spotted LeGendre who possessed the most photogenic features and Nat Pendleton, the wrestler, who portrayed, tough characters and wrestled with lions on the screen.

Undoubtedly, the Paris Games of 1924 were a splendid success and had more than atoned for the shabby show of two decades ago. Excellent performing conditions helped the competitors establish 24 Olympic and 11 world records. The Americans garnered most of the medals but Finland maintained the pressure. The French carried the day in Fencing and Cycling and Sweden continued its predominance in the Modern Pentathlon.

Stockholm saw the introduction of Art competitions in the Olympics programme and Paris accorded them full recognition with higher standards set so that none could qualify for a prize in music and the first place in architecture went abegging.

19

AMSTERDAM 1928
Olympics of Nany 'Firsts'

In the absence of Queen Withelmina, who was paying a visit to Norway, Prince Hendrik presided over the opening ceremony of the IX Olympic Games in Amsterdam on Saturday, July 18. As a mark of respect to the Ancient Games, the Greek delegation was given precedence to lead the march past of competing nations. (A convention has since developed that the Greek delegation always leads the march past in the opening ceremony of the Olympic Games). One of the Dutch athletes took the Olympic oath on behalf of all the competitors. As the Olympic flag was run up on the central mast a salute of guns was fired and thousands of pigeons were released from the cages which fluttered in the stadium for a while before speckling in the sky. Formal ceremonies over, the stage was set for the competitions to begin.

There was unbounded public enthusiasm. The 40,000 who managed to get admission were fortunate as an equal number, if not more, were trying in vain to get in because the new stadium was not spacious enough to accommodate any more. This aspect was not worth writing home about but for the ordeal the Finns had to undergo in getting entrance. They were almost lost in the jostling multitude outside and the rush around the portal was so great that they were scared stiff of a possible stampede. Unable to steer his team in, the panic stricken standard-bearer hit upon an unorthodox mode of entrance. He found it easier and expedient to scale over an outer wall and beckoned his team mates to follow suit. It sounds funny, but the official contingent from Finland stole into the stadium through unauthorised route for the opening ceremony! The American team had also experienced the same predicament but they managed to gate crash their entry.

In retrospect, the Finns and the Americans must have thanked their stars in matters concerning entry into the stadium on the opening day. The French were not so lucky; they were insulted and humiliated, too. Ultimately, they could not get entrance and were conspicuous by their absence during the opening ceremony. It so happened that on the previous day, the French team wanted to have a look at the arrangements inside the stadium but was barred by the gate keeper in offensive and insulting manner. Aggrieved, the French sought official intervention whereupon there were apologies galore and the matter compromised on the assurance that the errant gate-keeper would be dismissed. But when the French came for the opening ceremony the next day they were confronted with the same gate-keeper who was still very much there performing his functions non-challantly. This was in clear violation of the assurances given by the organisers the previous day and the French, who did not prefer a repeat of the confrontation, retreated without participation in the opening ceremony. Profuse apologies, however, hushed up the incident in time so that the French athletes were back to participate in the actual competitions later.

Three events were finalised on Sunday, July 29, the first day of the competitions. Burly John Kuck of the USA put the weight to an Olympic and world record distance of 52 ft. 0/13/16 inch (15.87 metres) to win a gold. Also of the USA was Robert King who leapt 1.94 metres to claim the top spot in the high jump. The great event, however, was the 10,000 metres race in which there was Paavo Nurmi once again to proclaim his superiority with a timing of 30 min. 18.8 secs. Ville-Ritola, who kept him company throughout was only a fraction of a second behind.

The second day of the competitions was to witness the first stunning surprise of the sprint programme at Amsterdam. That was in the 100 metres dash in which an absolutely unknown athlete from Canada, 19-years old high school student, Percy Williams, jumped the pack and pounded in ahead of the reputed field of runners in 10.8 secs. To be sure, the youngster's sensational performance was neither a fluke nor a flash in the pan. Two days later, i.e., on Wednesday, August 1, he sprinted down the half lap like a whirl wind to breast the tape two feet ahead of Great Britain's Walter Rargeley in the 200 metres event in 21.8 secs. He thus achieved the unique distinction of a grand 'double' winning the two short sprints in the same Olympics, a performance matched by only two athletes till then: — Archie Hahn did it in 1904 and Ralph Craig in 1912.

The day Percy Williams shot his way through the 100 metres, two more events produced results which were significant for another reason also. Till then, the USA had never lost the 400 metres hurdles and the hammer throw events. The monopoly in 400 metres hurdles was broken first by David Lord Burghley of Great Britain who beat Frank Cuhel and Morgan Taylor of the USA by a fraction of a second and then in the hammer throw event by genial giant, youthful Dr. Patrick O'Calleghan of the Irish Free State who hurled the weight farthest to beat the best effort of Ossian Skold of Sweden by four inches.

A pack of six great middle distance runners of the time assembled on the starting line of the 800 metre final on Tuesday, July 31, that included record breakers Lloyd Hahn of the USA and Sera Martin of France besides Doughlas Gordon Love, winner at the last Olympics. Looking back at the records, no other athlete till then had won any race short of 10,000 metres at two successive Olympic Games, and then at 10,000 it was no other than the super-human Paavo Nurmi. If that was any pointer, then Lowe stood no chance.

A brisk pace was set by Lloyd Hahn from the start — but too fast to last for two laps. Sera Martin and Phil Edwards, who committed the mistake of trying to match the pace in the initial stages, found themselves spent up for the final dash but Lowe was shrewd enough to have reserved enough steam for the burst at the opportune moment and startled and dazzled everybody with the speed at the finishing line, ahead of the great field in a new record time of 1 min. 51.8 secs. Douglas Lowe not only bettered the 16-years old record of James Meredith but also became the first athlete to win a middle distance race in two consecutive Olympic Games.

Another 16-year-old record broken that day was in the long jump when Edward B. Hamm of the USA jumped 7.73 metres laterally to improve upon Albert Gutterson's distance by 13 cms.

The Finns kept up the tradition of excelling in the long distance races as usual. Nurmi, now past 30 years, was no more unbeatable, his success in the 10,000 metres notwithstanding. But if it was not Nurmi, there was always some other Finn to hold aloft his country's banner; Harri Larva, a pupil of Nurmi showed tenacity and great fighting qualities in overhauling the French ace, Jules Ladoumegue, who had taken a sizable lead 300 metres from the finishing line. Larva got the gold medal with a new Olympic record time of 3 min. 53.2 secs.

The Finns made a clean sweep of the 3,000 metres steeple chase event. Toivo Loukola pared a full 12 secs. off the existing record of Ville Ritola to win in a new record time of 9 min. 21.8 secs. with Paavo Nurmi second and Ove Anderson third. In the 5,000 metres Ville Ritola avenged his defeat of 1924, clocking in 14 min. 38 secs. He had Nurmi trailing a full 8 secs. behind him with Edvin Wide of Sweden breathing over Nurmi's shoulders to finish third. The races in which Nurmi and Ritola were grimly fighting for supremacy were the highlights of the Games.

In addition to the long distance races, the Finns exhibited their superiority in the decathlon event also. Paavo Yrjola with an Olympic and world record tally of 8053.29 points bagged the gold medal beating the existing record of Harold Osborn by 343 points. Another Finn, Akilles Jarvinen, was second with 7931.50 points.

The hop, step and jump event threw up an Olympic winner for the first time from the 'Land of the Rising Sun'. Mikio Oda not only won a gold medal for Japan in the field events but also set a precedence of monopolising this particular event of triple jump in the next two Olympic Games with record breaking performances by the Japanese athletes.

On the last day of the track and field events, 75 runners from 24 nations lined up for the start of the great marathon race. A dark skinned Algerian named A.B. Elquafi, serving as an auto mechanic in Paris, won a trying race for France in 2 hrs. 32 mins. 57 secs. after having badly trailed in the initial stages of the 42,195 metres course. He was in a comparatively better shape at the finish to respond to the cheering crowd and the salute of the guard of honour that was presented to him. Much more effusive, ebullient and exuberant was the Chilean Miguel Plaze who even on finishing second, grabbed his country's flag, held it aloft and made an extra lap of the track.

A notable feature of the Amsterdam Games was the loss of supremacy of US in the track and field events which they had hitherto enjoyed. Barring the 400 metres flat race won by Raymond Barbutti and the two relay races, the USA yielded to foreign challenge in all the remaining races. In the field events, too, there were no sweeping victories but together with a good haul of gold in the swimming events, both men and women, they were just enough to enable the USA to retain the overall unofficial championship. Finland continued to hold sway in the long distance races and coupled with victories in the decathlon was staking its claim for supremacy in the world of sports. Compared to the eight gold medals in the track and field events for the USA, with a population of about 12 crores in the late twenties, the bag of 5 gold medals by Finland with only 35 lakh inhabitants was indeed a signal achievement. Germans, participating for the first time after 1912 for they were not invited to the 1920 and 1924 Games as a penalty for acts of commission and omission during the first world war, violating the tenets of international peace and amity and unleashing the source of global war on the world in 1914, made an impressive showing finishing third among the leading nations. The gymnasts from Switzerland picked up five gold medals to earn a name for their country in the sphere of sports. France and Italy fought out the fencing events in an exciting series of matches.

A new peak in the Olympic organisation was now reached. A record number of 3,015 contestants, including 290 of the fair sex, hailing from 46 countries, participated in the Games at Amsterdam to make it the most representative Olympic meet till then. The number of different nations which shared the prizes rose to twenty seven. For the first time track and field and gymnastic events were thrown open for women. Till then, their participation was restricted to fencing, swimming, tennis, archery and skating. Five track and field events for women, viz., 100 metres, 800 metres, 4 × 100 metres relay, high jump and discus throw, were gone through in all of which new Olympic and world records were created which, coupled with the new standards seen in the swimming events, were largely responsible for the 24 Olympic and 14 world records that were set at Amsterdam. In gymnastics for women, only one team competition was held in which women from Netherland excelled.

It was here at Amsterdam that India scored its first win in the Olympic Games. In the final of the field hockey, they trounced Netherlands 3.0. It was the first of the five successive wins India was destined to score in the Olympic Games. India, then under British rule, fielded mostly, Anglo-Indians players in the final match. Only two native Indians played in the final match. A look at the composition of the first victorious Indian team will be not without interest. The team was RJ Allen, ME Rocque, LC Hammond, RA Norris, BE Pinniger, MA Cullen, MA Gately, GE Marthins, FS Seaman, Dhyan Chand and SM Yusuf.

Among the many firsts, the Olympic flame remained lighted throughout the run of the Games. A torch was lit at Olympia in Greece and carried by relays of runners to the stadium in Amsterdam to light the Olympic Flame. For the first time also, Baron de Coubertin, the founder of the Modern Olympic Games could not attend the Games due to illness. When Crown Prince Olav of Norway skippered his international 6-metre R-class Yacht "Norna" to victory, he was the first of the royal blood to have won laurels in the modern Olympic Games.

20

LOS ANGELES 1932
Records Shattering Games

If ever the profuse use of superlatives could be justified and the word record over played, it is in the context of the Olympic Games of 1932 held in Los Angeles. The layout of the Games left nothing to be desired, the amenities provided for the efficient conduct of the Games were perfect and the golden clime of California afforded an ideal setting. Even nature seemed to have lent a hand in making the X Olympics a strikingly memorable show as the weather continued to be so wonderfully pleasant as it had never been in any of the earlier Olympics. Old records tumbled with monotonous regularity, record crowds thronged the venue of the Games throughout and record receipts made the Games a record money spinner. And this last aspect needs to be viewed in its proper perspective.

When the stock market crashed in 1929, the world was plunged into a gloom by the great economic depression which continued to grip the world for more than a decade. Billionaires became paupers overnight, factories and plants were shut down and millions of people the world over were rendered jobless. Apprehensions were, therefore, not unfounded that the Californian community would neither find means to undertake such a big venture nor would the far-flung countries be able to fork out substantial sums needed to send their athletes to Los Angeles and the Games in 1932 were destined to be a flop. But the adage, 'if hopes were dupes, fears may be liars' proved true and notwithstanding the global gloom, the Games enjoyed an unparalleled success – the 'depression' could not depress the Olympic movement.

The State of California earmarked one million dollars for the Games, and the host city augmented it by issuing bonds worth 15 lakh dollars to make sure that monetary constraints did not stand in the way of making the Games a grand success. The enthusiastic organising committee made the best of the financial padding and were successful in staging the Olympic Games on a record breaking scale. The 1408 participants including 127 female athletes, representing 37 nations were dumbstruck by the pomp and grandeur of the arrangements. Being fully conscious of the fact that satisfactory lodging and boarding arrangements for the competitors and officials was half the battle won, the Americans had taken pains to make excellent arrangements in this regard. For them, an Olympic village was specially erected on the outskirts of the city spread over an area of 250 acres. It was an elaborate affair comprising 550 two-roomed cottages fitted with the latest amenities, including shower baths, some larger buildings were set apart for social get together where the athletes could also enjoy movies of their own events gone through during the day. Cuisine was equally taken well care of catering to the food habits and dietary preferences of the athletes of different nationalities. The women competitors were lodged in a posh hotel requisitioned exclusively for the purpose.

The Los Angeles Memorial Coliseum was converted into Olympic stadium with seating capacity for 1,05,000 spectators. A gem of a surface for the track and field events was developed inside it. Adjoining the main stadium, arenas were specially built for different sports: the Olympic auditorium for boxing and wrestling events which could be watched by 10,000 spectators; the swimming stadium with a 'dream' pool surrounded by cavalcadic stairs specious enough to hold 12,000 viewers; a rowing course on Alamitos Bay along which there was a seating arrangement for 17,000 and standing room for spectators twice over; a firing range for shooting events in a secluded area where the participants may not be vexed by possible trespassers; Tennis courts, Roque courts, Art Museum, etc., besides scores of playgrounds and open areas placed at the disposal of the visitors for practice. For the first time, the facilities were truly functional which largely contributed to the creation of many records. The time measuring devices used were accurate to one hundredth of a second.

All told, the performing conditions and arrangements for the creature comforts of the competitors were simply marvelous and an all-time high was reached in the realm of organisation. In terms of numbers, however, the participation of countries was admittedly on the low side but that was quite understandable as a corollary to long distances involved and pecuniary problems flowing from the world wide economic depression. Even so, those who were lucky enough to make the trip to Los Angeles and those who were not so fortunate, were all living symbols of the big leap forward that the Olympic movement had taken by then. The zeal and alacrity with which the Brazilian team set sail, no matter if the entire team was not destined to reach its goal, is a case in point. Badly short of liquid money, but ever so hell- bent to participate in the Games, the Brazilian government loaded fifty thousand bags of coffee on an idle naval ship and gave the green signal to its 69 member contingent with the adjuration, that the expenses to be incurred in Los Angeles might be met from the sale proceeds of the consignment to be sold at the ports enroute. Prima facie, it was a master plan in those days of depressed economy. But as it turned out, there were few buyers at the ports touched so that Brazil's staple product could earn sustenance allowance for only one-third of its contingent for their sojourn in Los Angeles. The remaining two-thirds had to return home after a long outing on the high seas without setting foot on the Californian soil.

It was an election year in the USA and in the absence of President Herbert Hoover who was pre-occupied with his election campaign for a second term at the White House, Vice-President Charles Curtis presided over the opening ceremony of the X Olympic Games on Saturday, July 30 and declared the Games open with the words: "In the name of the President of the United States, I proclaim open the

Olympic Games of Los Angeles". A seething mass of humanity, estimated at well over a lakh, had jampacked the huge stadium to witness the spectacular ceremony at which cannons roared to herald the beginning of the Games and thousands of pigeons were released to carry the message of peace to far off places. Lt. George Calnan of the US, a bronze medalist at the 1928 Olympic games in the individual epee event of fencing competitions, took the Olympic oath on behalf of all the competitors.

The day's festivities concluded with some preliminary rounds in several sports. George Calnan died within a year in the Akron airship disaster on April 6, 1933.

Competitions in track and field events commenced the following day, i.e., Sunday, July 31. Three events were decided each going to a different nation and the ferocity of the contests witnessed in the heats of the 100 metres and 400 metre hurdles gave a foretaste of the record breaking spree that was to be the order of the day during the following week. In his last attempt in shot put, the burly New York youngster, Lee Sexton tossed the weight to an Olympic record distance of 16 metres to win the first event on the programme. In the next event even if no new height was reached, the result was particularly singular. Except Con Leahy of Ireland who had won the high jump event in the 1906 unofficial Games, no other jumper had ever outshone the USA in this particular discipline. Duncan McNaughton of Canada did it with a leap of 1.97 metres and clinched the issue in the jump-off. So hotly was this event contested that besides McNaughton, three other athletes cleared 1.97 metres and all the four were tied at that height so that all the places were decided in the jump-off.

Even more surprising upset was in the 10,000 metres race which had been the sole preserve of the Finns. Of course, Nurmi and Litola were not there as their amateur status had been challenged but in Volmari Iso-hollo and Lauri Virtanen of Finland had two worthy successors to its outgoing aces at long distance. But Janusz Kusocinski of Poland, an absolute stranger, seemed to be bent upon making a dent in the Finn monopoly and that he did. The race was run on a very fast pace throughout and no wonder that the first three, Kusocinski, Iso-Hollo and Virtanen in that order, dwarfed the record breaking efforts of the great Paavo Nurmi four years back. A new Olympic record which was 7.4 seconds faster than the previous best was set.

In the heats of the 100 metres, the eight years old record of 10.6 secs. was twice shattered. First, Arthur Jonath of Germany clipped one-tenth of a second and soon thereafter the be-spectacled Negro from USA, Eddie Tolan, dashed down in 10.4 secs. Similarly on the very first day of the competitions Lord Burghley's record of 53.4 secs. for the 400 metres hurdles was beaten by Both Tisdall of Ireland and Glenn Hardin of the USA. But these records did not last even 24 hours and were eclipsed the following day.

The six finalists that toed the mark for the 100 metres dash were a bunch of such speedy runners that even Percy Williams, the double sprint winner at the previous Games, was outsprinted in the semi-finals itself. After a false start, the pack jumped off and swept away like a hurricane so that all the first three, Eddie Tolan, Ralph Metcalf and Arthur Jonath in that order broke the existing record. Tolan and Metcalf both tied at 10.3 secs. world record but the judges picked Tolan as the winner, which was later confirmed by the photo finish cameras and electro-photographic timer. Jonath of Germany on the third spot was only a fraction of a second behind but even his time of 10.4 secs. was one-fifth of a second faster than Harold Abraham's record of 10.5 secs. set in Paris eight years ago.

The 200 metres short sprint provided a more exhilarating fare. The existing record of 21.6 secs. set by Archie Hahn in 1904, even though equalled once by Jackson Scholz in 1924, had stood for 28 years but in the heats on August 2 and the final on August 3 it was shattered seven times. First it was Metcalfe who pared one tenth of a second. Soon Tolan equalled the new time and before long Carios Binachi Luti of Argentine clipped another fraction of a second which in turn was immediately equalled by Jonath of Germany.

When such record breaking stalwarts crouched on the starting mark for the final on August 3, suspense was at its zenith and excitement ran high. But in 21.2 secs. Eddie Tolan transformed the state of suspense into one of admiration and amazement when he sprinted the half lap in a flash to set up a new Olympic record and became the fastest human runner on earth. He was the only athlete who had the unique distinction of being double winner in Los Angeles.

The most sensational of the track events was, however, the 5,000 metres race which could be termed the piece-de-resistance of the 1932 Games. As it turned out, it almost triggered a controversy but for the timely and intelligent handling of the situation by the organisers.

Ever since the days of Hannes Koleshmainen, the Finns had always hit the headlines in the long distance races. At Los Angeles Lauri Lahtinen and Lauri Virtanen were there to maintain the tradition and were staking their country's claim in the 5,000 metres race. The USA has had no credentials to offer in longer races, particularly beyond 1,500 metres, but for the first time at Los Angeles they had a potential challenger in the person of Ralph Hill of Oregon. Of the 14 starters, Lehtinen, Hill and Virtahen soon forged ahead and the three remained closeted in that order for 11 laps, after which Virtanen started showing unmistakable exhaustion and staggered behind. That left Lehtinen leading with Hill almost breathing at his shoulders. In this position, both of them entered the final stretch and started accelerating the pace for the final spurt with the finishing line in sight. In the final thundering down the stretch, Hill seemed to gain over his rival but as he tried to swing out towards right for going ahead, Lehtinen also swung out forcing Hill to stay behind. Hill then tried to switch over to the inside lane to forge ahead but Lehtinen also swerved towards left which apparently check mated Hill who could not thus cross him. In this grim struggle for supremacy both of them pounded down on the finishing line and breasted the tape together in the record time of 14 mins. 30 secs. For the naked eye it was a dead heat but the electro photographic timer picked Lehtinen a shade ahead of Hill.

The announcement of the result gave rise to a terrific furore as the 60,000 strong crowd was a witness to the deliberate and wilful obstruction caused by Lehtinen in a desperate bid to block and impede Hills passage so that he might not surge past. From full throated booings, catcalls and threatening postures, the massive disapproval of Lehtinen's malfeasance could have assumed dangerous proportions but for some intelligent quick witted officials incharge of the public address system who nipped the trouble in the bud by a very shrewd and tactful appeal. "Remember, please, these people are our guests". It had the desired effect, the rising discontent immediately calmed down and there was a spontaneous applause for the heroic performance of the athletes.

This incident apart, it certainly was a great race. It sounds incredible that over a distance of well over three miles, two athletes ran neck and neck and ultimately finished in dead heat and that, too, in a record time. The feat speaks volumes of the grit and stamina of the two runners.

Another outstanding race was the 400 metres in which the rivalry between William Carr and Benjamin Eastman, both of USA, who finished first and second respectively, was responsible to a great extent in generating enough heat and excitement so that this event also went in the record books as one of the most memorable races. Carr was the reigning champion of the race. Eastman's preserve was the 800 metres but he was good enough in the one-lap-sprint-cum-stamina race, too. Mutual rivalry egged Eastman to drop out from 800 metres and instead contest the 400 metres to square his earlier defeats at Carr's hand. In the earlier stages of the race, no assessment could be made because of the staggered starts but at the start of the final stretch Eastman with long strides seemed to have an edge. But Carr was true to what he was known for. In the last 60 metres be teared along in a fierce closing sprint and by the time he breasted the tape he had already pulled away a neat 2 metres ahead of his rival, returning in an Olympic and world record timing of 46.2 secs. The existing record of 47.6 secs. was set by Rev. Eric Liddle in 1924 at Paris and the fact that even Alexander Wilson of Canada who finished third, eight metres behind, also broke this eight years old record would make one marvel of the great exhibition of running that must have been on view.

William Carr later anchored his country's team to win gold medal in the 4 x 400 metres relay race in an Olympic and world record time of 3 min. 8.2 secs.

When Carr's superb graceful performances on the cinderpath are remembered, one can't help recalling the tragedy that betook him within eight months of his record breaking triumph in the Olympics. Poor Carr, still a junior in college and having plenty of sprinting years ahead, was involved in an auto-accident in which he suffered fracture of both the legs incapacitating him for life. The poor boy could not run any more.

Talking of tragedies that struck Olympic heroes brings to mind the premature demise of another champion, George Salling, the brilliant timber topper of the USA, nine months after his record shattering victory in the 110 metre hurdles at Los Angeles.

The concluding event was the marathon race which was won by a 20-year old newsboy, Juan Carlos Zabala from Argentine, in a record time of 2 hours 31 mins. 36 secs. It is said that Zabala had confidently foretold that he was going to win the race and it proved that it was no idle boast. His time was a full one minute better than that of Hannes the 'Mighty' which had stood for the last 12 years. But the remarkable feature of this traditionally prestigious race was that for the first time four runners were jogging around the track in the stadium at the same time and the first four runners were all home within the existing record time. Samuel Ferris of Great Britain was only 19 seconds behind Zabala and Arms Toivonen of Finland only 17 secs. behind Ferris.

Out of the 23 track and field events for men, 18 Olympic records were created, 9 of which were also world records. In fact, it is earlier to recount the four events in which old records did not get a beating. But interestingly, if time or distance in those events were not outstanding enough to be remembered, some peculiar incidents got associated to make them memorable, too. For instance, in the

3,000 metre steeplechase, an error unique in the history of the Olympic Games was committed. Due to inadvertance and sheer negligence on the part of the officials in charge, the competitors were made to run one extra lap. Thus, instead of 3,000 metres, they actually ran 3,450 metres. For the winner, Volumari Iso-Hollo, it made no difference as he led all the way and would have won whenever the race was stopped. But the results of the second and third places would have reversed as Joseph McCluskey of the USA was at second place when the race should have ended but Thomas Evenson occupied the second spot when the race actually ended after an extra lap. As for the record, Iso-Hallo in all probability must have established a new one as in the heats he had clocked 9 min. 14.6 secs. which was a neat 7 seconds faster than the existing record of Taivo Loukola. Of course, Iso-Hallo had his chance four years later in Berlin, where he proved his worth in no uncertain manner.

Another event was the hammer throw in which no new distance was achieved. But incidentally this was the only event in the Games at Los Angeles in which the champion of the previous Olympics, Dr. Patrick O'Callaghan, defended his title successfully.

New Olympic and world records were hoisted in all the six athletic events for women. Mildred Didrikson of the USA was the heroine of the Games with first places in 80 metre hurdles and the javelin throw and a silver medal in the high jump. In women's swimming, four Olympic and three world records were created and of the total seven events, six were claimed by the USA, the solitary exception being the 200 metres breast stroke won by Clare Dennis of Australia in an Olympic record time of 3 min. 6.3 secs.

Japan emerged as the leading swimming nation and had the lion's share in winning five of the eight swimming events for men. Sweden continued its firm hold on the modern pentathlon event as did India in the field hockey. India's goal getting spree on way to winning the championship struck dumb the sporting world. Runners-up Japan was beaten by eleven goals to one in the final and in the semi-final India had trounced the USA by 24 goals to one, unbelieveable but-true.

In the 1928 India team, there were only two native Indians. The team in 1932 was comparatively more representative. The eleven who played in the final against Japan were S.M. Jaffar, Roop Singh, Dhyan Chand, Gurmit Singh, Khullar, RJ Carr, SJS Bokhari, B.E. Pinniger, MAK Minhas, LC Hammond, CC Tapsell, and AC Hind.

The USA won the overall unofficial championship so convincingly that there was no serious challenger worth the name. But a salient feature which stood out in her major success was the predominance of coloured athletes who filled the ranks in good numbers.

The ideal conditions at Los Angeles brought out the best in the competitors whose performances were of an exceptionally high order so that one can hardly resist the temptation to get lyrical in their praise. Undoubtedly, the 1932 Olympic Games were by far the most exciting and successfully staged till then and were marked by a degree of sportsmanship worthy of emulation, thus securing the Olympic movement for all times to come.

21

BERLIN 1936
Perfection Attained

The high water-mark reached in organisational skill and athletic performance in Olympic Games were thoroughly eclipsed at Berlin. In keeping with traditional German thoroughness, the Games were, indeed, the best organised and most magnificent ever held. The athletic grounds and arenas were by far the finest ever prepared for Olympic competition. To think that all this excellence and perfection was achieved at a time when the world was beset with political problems — problems of the magnitude which had rendered the world seething with national hatred and which were indicating in no uncertain manner that the outbreak of a world-wide conflagration was hard at hand….!

It was the time when Adolf Hitler had attained supreme command after successfully weathering all political upheaval in Germany and was fully set to exercise his dominating influence in world affairs and mould the destiny of the humanity for good or bad. To achieve this, the first pre-requisite, doubtless, was to project an impressive and benevolent image of the Nazi Germany and Hitler was quick to uptake the golden opportunity that the hosting of the Olympic Games afforded. No cost or sacrifice was considered too great for the purpose. No matter, therefore, if the estimated outlay was to the tune of thirty million dollars, provided, of course, the new Germany won the admiration of the world community into the bargain.

And true to salt, the Germans gave such a superb display of their competence and thoroughness that even the veterans of the earlier Olympic Games were struck dumb at the sight of the Berlin set-up that was unfolded. The amenities provided at the luxurious Olympic village, only 15-kilometres from the main stadium, were a definite improvement over those at Los Angeles. There were 150 cottages spread over an area of 136 acres; each cottage distinguished by the name of a German city, artistically and tastefully decorated and spacious enough to house 20 men; the complex was equipped with all modern conveniences — library, hospital, swimming pool, theatre, etc. There was also plenty of open space for limbering and loosening up of athletes in their practice sessions. Scores of energetic volunteers and willing youngsters were always at hand to serve as errand boys, guides and interpreters for the multi-lingual athletes drawn from all parts of the world.

The main Olympic stadium, where the opening ceremony and the track and field events were to be held, had a seating capacity for 1,10,000 spectators. There were eight other arenas for competitions in other disciplines and all in all, there was seating arrangement for a total of 2,37,000, not to speak of the standing room for spectators many times over. The swimming stadium alone could hold 18,000 spectators at a time and the nearby Deutschland Hall, venue of the wrestling, weight-lifting and boxing events was spacious enough for 20,000 spectators.

To shut out the surging crowds and the over enthusiastic spectators from intervening the narration every now and then, let it be said that the enthusiasm of the overflowing crowds had surpassed all records. Braving the inclement weather which plagued the Games throughout, there was always a seething mass of humanity filling the various arenas to the brim even while heats and minor competitions were in progress. It was as if the German citizenry had gone crazy during the Olympic fortnight. They would flock in to witness any thing and every thing which was being dished out in the name of the Olympics even if they were totally stranger to the rudiments. An exhibition baseball game between two amateur American teams drew one lakh spectators! Altogether, nearly 45 lakh tickets were sold fetching a cash return as high as 28 lakh dollars which was way-ahead of the highest income derived from the Olympic Games till then.

The German quest for a novelty resulted in an innovation which was not only spectacular but also recalled the Classical Age when the Olympic Games used to be accorded supreme reverence, bordering on religious sanctity. On July 21, ten days before the opening of the Games in Berlin, a solemn ceremony was held 1837 miles away. Attired in eye-catching ancient costumes to impart a touch of yore, a bevy of Grecian maidens assembled around the ruins of the Temple of Zeus, the original site of the Games in Olympia and with the help of a lens, converged the sun's rays to ignite a fire in an antique lamp thus rekindling the Olympic spirit from the land of its origin. With this sacred fire the magnesium torch held by a runner was lighted who started off towards Berlin. After about half a mile he was relieved by another runner and in this process of lighting one magnesium torch from the other repeated by a relay of some 3,300 runners running night and day; the Olympic flame lit in Olympia reached the venue of the Games passing through Greece, Bulgaria, Yugoslavia, Hungary, Austria, Czechoslovakia and Germany.

It was around noon on Saturday, August 1, when the spectacular opening ceremony was drawing to a close and some 3,000 pigeons, released from captivity were still fluttering around the stadium that the last of the torch-bearer, a white-clad runner, entered through the east gate, and with elegant, graceful strides on the track raced up the flight of steps leading to the marble basin on the top. He touched the ceremonial fire-front with his torch, and flames leapt amidst thunderous applause. The fire so lit continued burning until the Games ended on August 16.

Chancellor Hitler declared the Games open with the customary brief and simple sentence as provided in the Olympic code. Count Baillet-Latour, President of the IOC was at hand and Spiridon Louis, the winner of the marathon race in the first of the modern Olympic Games in 1896 at Athens, presented Hitler with an olive branch brought from Greece. The Olympic Oath on behalf of all the participants was taken by the German weight-lifter, Rudolf Ismayr, who had created an Olympic record in the middle weight division of the 1932 Games at Los Angeles.

On Sunday, August 2, the native spectators thronging the stadium had their fill of delight as their country won its first ever gold medal in the track and field events of the modern Olympic Games since 1896. The first event decided was the shot put in which Han Woellke of Germany tossed the weight to a new Olympic record distance of 16.20 metres. It is worthy of note that immediately after the Games were awarded to Berlin, enormous sums were spent on the training of German athletes and the extensive preparations were well repaid. Woellke was led before Herr Hitler who personally congratulated the winner. It was a soul-stirring triumph for the Nazi creed of Nordic supremacy and was therefore duly highlighted. It was praise worthy gesture on the part of a Head of a State to congratulate an Olympic winner but since the show-off was only to high light the racial supremacy of the Aryan race, of which the political pontiff was an staunch advocate, the otherwise laudable gesture was bound to land him in embarrassing situation sooner than he could imagine as victory or defeat in the Olympic Games was not to be guided by racial prejudices.

The next event was the 10,000 metre run which was a clean sweep for Finland. Ilrari Salminon breasted the tape in 30 min. 15.4 secs., only a metre ahead of Arvo Askola. Salminen, too, was brought before Der Fehrer. It was another matter that the warmth and spontaneity was lacking in the congratulations but it could pass out without making the news. However, soon the events that followed hit the headlines. The next event on the programme was the high jump which was a clean sweep for the USA but more importantly, Cornalius Johnson who cleared the bar at the Olympic record height of 2.03 metres as also David Albritton who was second, with only 3 cms. less, were both Negroes of the darkest tint. It was a rude jolt to Hitler's creed of Aryan supremacy and the best he could do was to leave the stadium abruptly in a huff.

The finals were decided on the second day of the competitions, i.e., Monday, August 3. In the first Karl Hein of Germany swang the hammer over his head several times before releasing the weight which landed 56.49 metres, a neat 1.75 metres farther than the record throw of M.J. McGarth of USA which had stood for the last 24 years. A deafening applause shook the stadium, more so as another German, Ervin Blask, won the second spot. Besides, as already stated, before these Games at Berlin, Germany had never won a single track and field championship, but within two days here they had bagged two 'golds' and a 'silver' and a 'bronze' to boot. Herr Hitler had, however, become wiser by now, and very prudently so. He exercised caution by avoiding public exhibition and congratulated Hein and Blask only in privacy. The caution soon paid rich dividends as his racial theory was exploded and blown sky high by the "black auxiliaries"[1] time and again during the Games. In the result, his personal image would have been badly tarnished if he had congratulated only the 'white' winners and ignored the black ones.

The star attraction that second day, as it is ever and anon, was the 100 metres race in which Jesse[2] Owens, Ralf Metcalfe and Mykoff of the USA, Hans Strandberg of Sweden, Erich Borchmeyer of Germany and Nartinus Osendarp of the Netherlands toed the mark for the finals. Drenched by occasional downpours, the track was soggy but except Metcalfe, the rest of the bunch exploded at the bark of the gun. Owens, usually not a fast starter, was off the mark quickly and sped down the track in a flash ahead of the rest to equal the Olympic and world record time of 10.3 secs. established by Eddie Tolan in Los Angeles four years ago. Metcalfe, handicapped by a bad start, sprinted in great style overtaking and cutting down the early lead of all his rivals except, of course, Owens. Metcalfe was second in 10.4 secs. and Martinus Osendarp only a metre behind him at the third spot. With the first two on the victory stand being of the dark hue, the Nazi's racial theory and political creed of Nordic supremacy received a rude jolt. But it was only the beginning, and behold, the following day was Tuesday, — Black Tuesday for Hitler's racial article of faith.

There were three finals – 800 metres flat, long jump and 400 metres hurdles listed for the day besides heats in 200 metres race. The weather was bleak and murky and the air raw but the spectacular performances turned out by the 'black auxialiaries' led by Owens, the Tan streak from Ohio, warmed and cheered up the vast multitude to the heights of ecstasy. During the day, he surpassed the former Olympic records four times and the world record twice.

Paradoxically enough, whereas Owen's victory in the long jump was just in keeping with the popular expectations, a situation had arisen in the qualifying rounds when his elimination from the event at the preliminary stage seemed a distinct possibility. Almost immediately after his sensational, world record-breaking timing of 21.1 sec. in the trial heats of the 200 metres run, Owens headed towards the jumping pit where the qualifying rounds for the long jump event were in progress. To measure his run-up as also to test the surface beneath, he just strided down upto the take-off board without, of course, making a jump. But to his surprise he was shown the red flag by the judges indicating his running down the course had been counted and he had forfeited one of the three jumps that were allowed. In his second attempt he leapt well beyond the qualifying mark (23 ft. 5½ inches) with an apparent ease but to his dismay and surprise the red flag again went up on the ground that he had fouled by over-stepping the take-off mark. That left him with only one more chance and the greatest broad jumper of the world faced the grim possibility of being ousted from his specialised item just in case one of those mishaps recurred in the only chance left. Lutz Long, Germany's best bet in the long jump made a friendly advice to Owens that he should draw a line well behind the take-off board for his last jump. Owens followed the advice to the letter and the crisis was over.

In the finals that very afternoon, Owens leapt to a record distance of 7.87 metres in his second attempt which was equalled by Lutz Long in his fifth jump. But Owens immediately catapulated himself to a new Olympic record distance of 8.06 metres. It was the first time in the history of the Olympic Games that anybody had ever soared in the air to cover eight metres. But Jesse's greatest performance was yet to come about which anon.

The 800-metres final was hotly contested and even though the ultimate winner's time was 3 secs. slower than Thomas Hompson's record set in Los Angeles, the race was astonishingly eventful. Nine renowned runners from seven countries had qualified for the final. Among them Woodruff of the USA was an abony-black young Negro who had the least experience of competitive running but was a member of the 'black-auxiliary' on account of his extraordinary talent which was yet to be proved. Before the race, Head Coach, Lawson Robertson, had advised the new find to surge past the pack right from the beginning and stay away from the 'crowd'. Woodruff, however, could not keep this tall order and soon found himself trailing at the rear of the pack. In his efforts to forge ahead, he found himself so badly mixed up in the bunch that it was almost impossible to dodge his way out. Thus, trapped, Woodruff could not contain his restlessness to get ahead in the lead beyond a lap. But as he was completely tangled and blocked by the jogging athletes in front, Woodruff ventured a desperate device. He just stopped running and came to a halt. This left him alone way back of the pack and for once free to set his own pace without any let or hindrance. Then he started galloping, throwing out his legs in great ground-covering-strides so that within 100 metres he not only cut down the lead he had conceded by coming to a full stop for a while but also out-paced the entire field of runners to sail along in front. This position, of course, he could not maintain for long as the Canadian Negro veteran, Dr Phil Edwards, breezed past him followed by Italy's best bet, Mario Lanzi, who also tore out in front. This left Woodruff once again trapped behind. But now that they were entering the final stretch, the earlier bizarre sort of strategy that he had adopted for disentangling himself would not work. Instead, he took a big leap in the fashion of the running long jump to overtake Lanzi and then sped past Edwards to hold the lead till the finish although Lanzi was making a desperate bid near the finishing line. It was a splendid race which shot to fame the raw, inexperienced Negro. Woodruff's time of 1 min. 52.9 secs., although not cast in the mould of the record-breaking spree in Berlin, was good enough when judged in the background of how he struggled to clear his path and had to make a detour in the process. Mario Lanzi finished second with Dr. Phillip Edwards third, both of whom were only a fraction of a second behind the winner.

But the greatest spectacle in sprinting was to be on view the next day, i.e., Wednesday, August 5, despite the bleakest weather — damp, cold wind blowing with continuous drizzles punctuated by intermittent showers. The unfavourable conditions and the soggy track, no doubt, could bog down even the best, but not the marvel of the cinder path and the hero of the Games at Berlin, Jesse Owens. With already two gold medals in his bag, he crouched on the starting block for the 200 metres dash along with team-mate Robinson, Osendarp and Wynand van Beveren of the Netherlands, Paul Haenni of Switzerland and Lee Orr of Canada, each stationed on their marks a few metres apart for the staggered start around the curve for the half a lap race. With the bark of the gun Jesse burst forth in front and sprinting with effortless grace, arms and legs working in perfect rhythm and piston like precision he glided around the curve so smoothly that even as the stretch began he had already a two metre lead over his nearest rival Robinson. On the flat, he pulled away a further three metres to breast the tape a clear 5 metres ahead in a world[3] record time of 20.7 secs. Mathew Robinson was home in 21.1 sec. for second place and Martinus Osendarp third in 21.3 secs.

The standing ovation that the 'Tan Streak from Chio State' received for such a grand exhibition of running which completed his triple triumph was well deserved. But the undisputed hero of the Berlin Games was yet to add another feather to his already well adorned cap. He was the lead-off sprinter of the USA quartet which won the 4x100 metre relay in an Olympic and world record time of 39.8 secs. And with four gold medals, Owens earned for himself a place in the rare company of Alvin Kraenzlein and Paavo Nurmi who achieved the unique distinction in the Olympic Games of 1900 and 1924 respectively. And even in this rare company, Jesse has a definite edge taking into consideration the keen competitions as also the ever increasing number of competitors. There were 893[4] athletes entered in the track and field events in Berlin which necessitated a good many additional qualifying heats and trials rendering the passage to the finals more strenuous and nerve raking.

With the victory in the triple jump on Thursday, August 6, Japan scored a hat-trick of winning the event in three successive Olympic Games. A worthy successor of Mikio Oda (1928) and Chuhei Nambu (1932) was Naoto Tajimo who kept up his country's eight years old tradition with an Olympic and world record distance of 16 metres. Another of the Nipponess, Masao Harada, was second with John Metcalfe of the USA placed third. This same day saw the emergence of a German athlete in the javelin throw event which had hitherto either been won by a Swede or a Finn. Gerhard Stoeck hurled the spear 71.84 metres away to win a 'gold' and sent the mammoth native crowd into raptures. But before the curtain fell on the day's programme, the 1,500 metre race was won by the slim New Zealander, Jack Lovelock, in an Olympic and world record time of 3 min. 47.8 secs. The race was so fiercely contested that besides the fleet-footed champion from down-under, four other runners, Jack Cunningham of USA, Luigi Beccali of Italy, San Romani of USA and Phil Edwards of Canada who finished in that order, all finished within the existing Olympic record time of 3 min. 51.2 secs. set by Beccali in 1932. It is rated as one of the great races in the track events of the Olympic Games as, of the 12 finalists comprising the world's greatest runners of the distance then, at least five of them at one time or the other during the run pulled away from their pursuers and led the pack. Finally, of course, it was the champion, Jack Lovelock, who had the last laugh.

The 5,000 metre long distance race on Friday, August 7, also bore the same classical mould in which all the first four finishers ran within the Olympic record time of 14 min. 30 secs. set by Lehtinen four years ago, Gunnar Hockert of Finland won the gold and established a new record time of 14 min. 22.2 secs. followed by countryman Lauri Lehtinen second and Sweden's Henry Jonsson third.

On the penultimate day of the track and field competitions, the USA made a clean sweep in decathlon with Glenn Morris scoring 7,900 points as per the revised table to set a new Olympic and world record. But the most attractive event of the day was the 3,000 metres steeple-chase in which Volmari Iso-Hollo of Finland covered the course in the new Olympic record time of 9 min. 3.8 secs. Incidentally, Iso-Hollo was the lone athlete in Berlin who successfully defended his title which he had won in Los Angeles, four years ago.

The marathon race, as usual, was run on the concluding day of the track and field events. There were 56 starters, including Juan Carlos Zabala, the defending champion, who went out on the course that led to the rural district along the Havel river and back. The entire course was lined by hordes of spectators and an estimated one million enthusiasts witnessed at least some part of the long distance race. Zabala gave up his efforts utterly exhausted after 32 kilometres of trundling. It was Kithel Son, the Korean born student of Tokyo University now representing Japan, who was crowned the new champion with an Olympic record time of 2 hrs. 29 min. 19.2 secs. Ernest Harper of Great Britain was second and another athlete from the Land of the Rising Sun, Shoryu Nan, third.

The Berlin Games were a record smashing success. A record number of 4,069 contestants including 328 of the fair sex representing 49 countries assembled for the greatest sporting show on earth in which 16 new Olympic records were created and one former record equaled. In the process, new world records were also established in five events. The champion in each discipline was awarded a gold medal, an Olive wreath and a small potted Oak tree as a living memorial of his outstanding performance in the Games. The USA led by the 'black-auxiliaries' once again asserted their supremacy in track and field events in unmistakeable terms. Of the 23 events, they annexed championship in 12; in other words, one more than the combined bag of the rest of the world. The unofficial team championship, however, rested with the host country. Germany, which had the largest representation in the Games, won 101 out of 420 medals. The overall German success was considerably boosted by their noteworthy wins in Gymnastics, Equestarian and Rowing events besides Boxing, Canoeing and Cycling.

The star of the women's track and field events was Helen Stephene of the USA who created an Olympic and world record of 11.5 secs. in the 100-metres dash. She also anchored the USA quartet in the 4 × 100 metre relay race to bring laurels to her team with yet another Olympic and world record time of 46.9 secs. and thus became the only double winner in the ladies section of the track and field.

The queen of the women's swimming was unquestionably Hendrika Mastenbrock of Netherlands who out-swam her rivals in the 100 and 400 metre free-style in the new Olympic record timings of 1 min. 5.9 secs. and 5 min. 26.4 secs. respectively. She also led her team to victory in the 4x100 metre relay besides winning a silver medal in the 100 metre back-stroke event.

In the team events, India, for the third time in succession, claimed the world's field hockey supremacy by trouncing Germany by eight goals to one in the final. More of the native Indians were progressively finding their way in the winning combination which was : Richard Allan, Carlyl Tapsell, Mohd. Hussain, Baboo Nimal, Cullen Goodsir, Joseph Galibardy, Shahabuddin, Shabban, Iqtidar Dara, Dhyan Chand, Roop Singh, Syed. Mohd. Jaffer and Ali Shah.

Having being champions in Amsterdam (1928) and Los Angeles (1932) Olympics, India were the hot favourites in Berlin. But German interest had suddenly aroused consequent upon a 4-1 victory over India in a practice match on Indian's arrival in Berlin. In the final, however, India thrashed Germany 8 – 1 with Dhyan Chand, playing barefooted, netting six spectacular goals. The trio of Dhyan Chand (center forward), brother Roop Singh (left in) and Syed Mohd. Jaffer (left out) was irresistible.

Hitler, who witnessed the match was so baffled and astonished by the amazing stickwork and dazzling ball control of the Indians that he is stated to have confided with his aides if it would be worthwhile to investigate the possibility of Indians having some sort of magnet planted in their hockey sticks....!

22

POST WORLD WAR II
Games Continue Roaring

Soon after the Olympic flame flickered and died in the ceremonial fire-front on the top of the stadium in Berlin, political developments on the continent as also in far east were rather swift. Japan soon realised that its entanglement with China was one too many to think of any exercise in matters unconnected with the twin questions of war and peace and in mid 1938 informed the IOC about its inability to host the 1940 Olympic Games in Tokyo. Thereupon, the IOC immediately assigned the Games to Helsinki and the Finnish Organising Committee set about the task in right earnest. But the war flames out-paced the Olympic flame so that before the Olympic flame could be lighted in Helsinki in 1940, the Second World War erupted in 1939 and transformed the sporting instincts in man into his most unsportsmanlike activity. Thus, the Games of the XII Olympiad, originally allotted to Tokyo and later to Helsinki, were consumed by the flames of the world war.

The mention of the fact that the XIII Olympiad to be held in 1944 was allotted to London and suffered the same fate can at best be of purely academic interest. Nonetheless, it certainly was one of the reasons which weighed heavily in favour of London when it came to selection of the venue for the 1948 Games.

Sigfrid Edstroem of Sweden had become the President of the IOC on the death of Count de Baillet-Latour in 1942. Immediately after the armistice, Edstroem summoned a meeting of the IOC executive committee in August 1945 in London to resurrect the Olympic movement. But the world was still licking the wounds inflicted by the blood bath and senseless slaughter perpetrated during the war. In the result, the response to Edstroem's call was none too encouraging as only Lord Aberdale of Great Britain and Avery Brundage of the USA turned up. But the trio, undeterred and undaunted, worked tirelessly and their efforts were crowned with success in reviving the Games in 1948.

Even after three years of the cessation of hostilities, Britain was still badly limping and groaning under the stress and strains of the war. London had yet to clear all the rubble from the aerial bombardment; essential commodities continued to be scarce and rationing was on; prices were soaring high and the Britishers were reeling under the heavy burden. In this backdrop, where austerity was the watchword, no flamboyance could be expected; nor could the Britishers afford to indulge in prodigality and ostentation to match the spectacle and splendour of the Berlin show of 1936. No new super-structures were raised, nor any innovations involving capital outlay undertaken. Whatever stadia and arenas existed in and around London were just given a face lift and they proved to be adequate enough.

Lord David Burghley, himself a distinguished athlete in his hey-days, having won gold medal in the 400 metre hurdles in the Olympic Games at Amsterdem in 1928, headed the British Olympic Association and contrived to make the best of whatever was available and an exquisitely impressive show was the result.

Invitations were extended to all the member nations of the IOC, except, of course, Germany and Japan — the two arch enemies of the allies in the recently concluded world war. Italy, Austria, Hungary and Rumania, the countries which had also lined-up against the allied forces, though were, however, welcome and were among the 59 countries which were represented by a record number of 4,468 competitors, including 438 women contestants.

If monetary constraints did not permit extravagance and pomp and show, the British organisers made up for the lack by dramatizing some minute details and novel features. Twelve days before the formal opening of the Games, the sun's rays were focused on a piece of olive wood in front of the Temple of Zeus in Olympia to ignite it. With the fire so produced, an ancient lamp was lit and the flames preserved until a Greek soldier, 23-year old Constantine Dimitretis, appeared in full armour. In utmost reverence, sanctifying ancient Greek traditions, the soldier shed his martial apparel and surrendered his gun, thus transforming himself from a soldier into an athlete. He then lit a torch from the ancient lamp and set out on the first leg of the journey towards London.

Thus, the Olympic movement got the better of the world conflagration and continued as under:-

Olympiad	***Year***	***Venue***
14th	1948	London
15th	1952	Helsinki
16th	1956	Melbourne
17th	1960	Rome
18th	1964	Tokyo
19th	1968	Mexico
20th	1972	Munich
21st	1976	Montreal
22nd	1980	Moscow
23rd	1984	Los Angeles
24th	1988	Seoul
25th	1992	Barcelona
26th	1996	Atlanta
27th	2000	Sidney
28th	2004	Athens
29th	2008	Beijing
30th	2012	London
31st	2016	Rio de Janeiro

All these Games are fully documented both in print as also on celluloid.

It is significant to note that the Olympic Games having been revived in 1896 AD after 1500 years of suspension since 393 AD, retained its name which it carried since 776 BC – “The Olympic Games”.

References

1. The ten Negro athletes of the track and field squad of the USA were rather slightingly referred to in the Nazi newspapers as “The black auxiliaries”.
2. James Cleveland Owens was his real name. But when he first went to school and the teacher asked his name, Owens simply replied “J.C.” (the first two initials). To the teacher it sounded ‘Jesse’ and from thence on, the all time great athlete is known as Jesse Owens.
3. The world record for 200 metres on the straight away was 20.6 seconds and 21.2 secs. around a turn. Nobody had ever clocked even 21 secs. along a curve. Owens’ fantastic time was within one-tenth of a second of the world record on a straight course.
4. This was three times the number of competitors in the track and field events at Los Angeles in 1932.

Index

E

F

G

H

I

J